BABIES NAMES
A - Z

by

André Page

PAPERFRONTS
ELLIOT RIGHT WAY BOOKS
KINGSWOOD, SURREY, U.K.

Made and printed in Great Britain by
Richard Clay Ltd., Bungay, Suffolk.

BABIES NAMES
A - Z

Contents

Foreword

In addition to the well-known names in this book, I have also included a number of interesting but little known ones, from old records and documents. I have obtained a number of these and others from the Domesday book in The National Records Office in London, from old records at Somerset House, and from old books and documents in The British Museum.

I would like to express my thanks to the staff at all these places for their help and kindness on my visits.

ANDRÉ PAGE

This book has proved a great success, and this new edition has been revised by the author, and a number of new and rare names added.

A.P.

INTRODUCTION

Christian names were all that we had to define any particular person up to the time of William the Conqueror (A.D. 1066), for it was not until this time that surnames were used at all in Britain. Even up to the 14th century only a small proportion of the lower middle class had an hereditary surname (i.e. father and son) and it is doubtful if at that time 99% of the people could have written or spelt them, even if they had been given one.

THE 'ROYAL' CHRISTIAN NAMES

In these early days it was customary for many of the boys to be given Christian names similar to those of the reigning monarchs, and in a lot of cases these Christian names were Harold, William, Edward, Stephen and Richard - and these were handed down from father to son. When many people in any one town or village had the same Christian name, it was customary to refer to them by their trade, features, place of abode, or by a nickname, and then they might be referred to as William the Smith, William at the Wood or William of the Whitelock.

While there have been great changes over the years in the spelling of surnames - due to the fact that only very few people had even a modicum of learning - and that parish clerks would often write down the names of people as they sounded phonetically, there have not been so many changes in the spelling of Christian names. The list of Christian names - or 'forenames' - was at one time very small numerically, and it was not until the Normans, Anglo Saxons, Huguenots, Flemish weavers, Norsemen, the Danes, and many other people came to Britain, that we acquired the wealth of Christian names we have today.

POP OR SAINT?

Each decade brings a new batch of Christian names. Whereas in the olden times, Saints' names were often given to the children, today some get the names (or stage names) of pop, TV or sports stars. But is it fair to saddle a daughter with Toyah, Elkie or Kylie? Will a son in twenty years' time really be grateful that he was called Ringo, Alvin, Elton or even Bjorn? These are matters that readers must decide for themselves. In a case recently, the parents of a son had him christened with all the eleven Christian names of the local football team which they supported. Is he going to be grateful for this when he grows up?

It is always tragic that some parents give their children Christian names which I am sure they would not like to have for their own, but a Mr Pepper who lived in Liverpool in 1880 wanted to make sure that his daughter would like at least 'one' of her Christian names, so he gave her twenty-six – one starting with every letter of the alphabet. These were: Anna, Bertha, Cecilia, Diana, Emily, Fanny, Gertrude, Hypatia, Inez, Jane, Kate, Louisa, Maud, Nora, Ophelia, Patricia, Quince, Rebecca, Susan, Teresa, Ulysses, Venus, Winifred, Xenophon, Yetty, Zeno Pepper. 'Quince' sounds a little 'fruity', and 'Yetty' was before they discovered the Abominable Snowman on Mount Everest, and I was always under the delusion that 'Ulysses' was a man's name, but in these days of unisex, who knows? It is to be hoped that Miss Pepper did not have to sign many legal documents during her lifetime. She must have been grateful however that her name was 'Pepper' and not 'Cholmondley-Marjoribanks'. But a gentleman later in the 18th century had the solution to this problem, and had his son christened 'Alphabet' Burrow.

THE POPULARITY COUNT

The frequency of Christian names has altered with the centuries. In the Domesday book for example, there is only one man named Nicholas, but a few named John, and not any with the names Philip or Thomas. In the 14th century William, Robert, Thomas and John accounted for about 80% of the boys' Christian names, and Margaret, Matilda, Cecilia, Joan, Alice and Agnes were the most common at this time.

A report a few years ago gave Elizabeth and James as the two most popular Christian names, and the next boys' names in order of popularity were Alexander, William, Thomas and John, and for the girls Louise was number two, followed by Jane, Mary and Sarah. It is possible that William and Harry may now be in the lead, in honour of Prince Charles' sons – with probably all the other Royal princes – Philip, Charles, Andrew and Edward all following closely. Similarly, after the birth of Prince Andrew's daughters, Beatrice and Eugenie may take over the top spots for girls' names.

But some parents do not keep to any of the traditional fore-names, and the Daily Telegraph a few years ago, had the following names in their Birth Announcement Columns: "Enk", "Leonline", "Piran" and "Terfion" for boys, and girls named "Aparna", "Maarat" and "Tayce". The origin of these are not known to me, and neither are the following names, which have been recorded in Parochial Registers, or in old documents in years past: Jeholada, Jachin, Elyarde, Barzillai, Dix, Richley, Sasso, Tine, Mariota, Elys, Shallum, Stine and Juet.

BIBLICAL NAMES

The Bible has given us a lot of our Christian names. 'Adam' and 'Eve' are two, but these were often given to the people who took these name parts in medieval religious processions. Some of the older generation people have been named Dorcas, Martha, Rebecca, Malachi and Philemon from the Bible. Puritan Christian names have included 'Bestedfast' Gunnings, 'Fear the Lord' Willard, and 'God is my salvation' Firth, but a man who lived in Yorkshire once had his four sons christened 'Do Well', 'Love Well', 'Die Well' and 'Fare Well'. The latter son did not 'fare' too well for he met his death by drowning!

ALTERATIONS AND DIMINUTIONS

The Christian names which rarely get altered are those of one syllable e.g. John, Jean, Rex, Rose and Clare, but others have a lot of variants. For example, Elizabeth and Elisabeth often get altered to Eliza, Elisa, Liza, Lisa, Liz, Lis, Lizzie, Elsie and Beth, and when Princess Margaret was very young she would call her sister – The Queen Elizabeth – 'Lillibet' – thus making but another variant of this name.

America has a number of 'exclusive' names, and these include, Otis, Wilbur and Elmer. Christian names have also originated from 'place' names, and these have included 'Lamorna' Birch (the famous artist), 'Barnes' Wallis (the noted designer) and 'Towyn' Thomas (the famous Welsh choir leader). 'Nick' names too have often been given to people who have certain surnames. These have included 'Dusty' Miller, 'Chalky' White, 'Tug' Wilson, 'Hooky' Walker and 'Nobby' Clark. Baldheaded men have sometimes attracted the name of 'Curly', and 'Lofty', 'Shorty' and 'Fatso' are not unknown.

The theatrical world has also managed to produce a few jokes on Christian names. These include: A friend saw a man walking down the road whose name was 'George Stinks', and he said to him, "Where are you going to, George?" George replied, "I am off to have my name changed by deed poll." His friend answered, "It is certainly not a pleasant sounding name. What are you changing it to?" George replied, "I am changing it to 'Fred Stinks' ". There is also the story of the man who was christened 'Charles "Damn It" Smith' because the vicar happened to stub his toe on the font when he was christening this boy.

If you do not like your own Christian name you can call yourself by any other name which pleases you, but in legal matters you must give your 'real' name. But do not worry too much what you are called, just as long as you do not get called too late for breakfast!

I hope that here you will be able to find Christian names for your children - and ones which you, and they - will still like when they grow up. Happy choosing!

BOYS' NAMES

Aaron: From the Hebrew 'Aharon', meaning 'most high'. Aaron was the brother of Moses.

Abel: From the Hebrew 'Hebel', meaning 'breath'. In the Bible, the second son of Adam was so called.

Abelard: From the Teutonic 'Adelhard' meaning 'resolute'.

Abiel: This name means a 'father of strength'.

Abner: From the Hebrew 'Abhner', meaning the 'father of light'. In the Bible, Abner was a cousin of Saul. This is a Christian name which is mainly used in America today.

Abraham: From the Hebrew 'Abram', meaning 'father of the people'. Variants are *Abe* and *Abie*. Example: *Abraham Lincoln*.

Adalbert: German for 'Albert', and meaning 'bright and noble'.

Adam: From the Hebrew, meaning 'formed of the red earth'. This name is mentioned in the Domesday book. Adam was the first man, and therefore this was the first Christian name.

Adamo: This is Italian for 'Adam', meaning 'formed of the red earth'.

Adan: Spanish for 'Adam', meaning 'formed of the red earth'.

Adao: Portuguese for 'Adam', meaning 'formed of the red earth'.

Adda: A Welsh form of 'Adam', meaning 'formed of the red earth'.

Adlai: From the Hebrew 'Adlai', meaning a 'witness'. Little used today.

Adolf: German for 'Adolph', meaning a 'noble warrior'.

Adolph: From the Germanic, meaning a 'noble warrior'.

Adolphe: French for 'Adolph', meaning a 'noble warrior'.

Adolpho: Both Italian and Spanish for 'Adolph', and meaning a 'noble warrior'.

Adolphus: Swedish for 'Adolph', and meaning a 'noble warrior'.

Adrian: A man who came from the area of the Adriatic.

Aelaro: Mentioned in the Domesday book of A.D. 1087. Maybe from 'Adalard', meaning 'noble'.

Aeneas: From the Greek, and meaning 'one who is praised'.

Agosto: Italian for 'Augustus', meaning 'majestic'.

Aidan: From the Gaelic, and meaning 'fiery'. Example St. Aidan.

Ailmer: Mentioned in the Curia Regis. A possible variant of 'Aylmer', meaning 'famous and noble'.

Ainsley: From this surname, and meaning 'one who lives by his own meadow'.

Alain: A French form of 'Alan', meaning 'in tune'.

Alan: From the Celtic 'Alan', and meaning 'in tune'. Variants are Allen, Allan and Alun.

Alaric: From the Teutonic, and meaning 'almighty ruler'.

Alarico: Spanish for 'Alaric', and meaning 'almighty ruler'.

Alastair: From the Gaelic 'Alexander', and meaning 'man's defender'.

Alban: From the Latin, and meaning 'white or fair'. Example: St. Alban, an English martyr of the 4th century.

Alberic: Swedish for 'Aubrey', and meaning 'blond ruler'.

Albert: From the Anglo Saxon 'Aethelbeorht', and meaning 'bright and noble'. Variants are *Bert, Bertie* and *Al*.

Alberto: Italian for 'Albert', and meaning 'bright and noble'.

Albin: From the Latin, and meaning 'one who is fair'.

Albrecht: German for 'Albert', and meaning 'bright and noble'.

Aldo: From the Teutonic, and meaning 'old'.

Aldous: From the Teutonic, meaning 'old'. This name is mentioned in the Hundred Rolls of A.D. 1273.

Aldred: From the Teutonic 'Aethelred', meaning 'mighty'. This name is mentioned in the Domesday book of A.D. 1087.

Aldus: A variant of 'Aldous' from the Teutonic, and meaning 'old'.

Alec: A diminutive of 'Alexander', and meaning 'defending man'.

Alessandro: Italian for 'Alexander', and meaning 'defending man'.

Alexander: From the Greek 'Alexandros', and meaning 'defending man'. Variants are *Alec, Sandy* and *Alex*. Examples: *Alexander the Great* and *Alexander Dumas*.

Alexandre: French for 'Alexander', and meaning 'defending man'.

Alexio: Portuguese for 'Alexander', and meaning 'defending man'.

Alexis: From the Greek, and meaning a 'helper'.

Alfred: From the Anglo Saxon 'Aelfred', meaning 'elf's counsel'. Variants are *Alf* and *Alfie*. Examples: *Alfred the Great* and *Lord Alfred Tennyson*.

Alfredo: The Italian and Spanish for 'Alfred', and meaning 'elf's counsel'.

Algernon: From the French, and meaning 'one who has whiskers'. Variants are *Algy* and *Algie*.

Alick: A variant of 'Alexander', meaning 'defending man'.

Alisdair: A Scottish form of 'Alexander', meaning 'defending man'.

Alistair: A Scottish form of 'Alexander', meaning 'defending man'.

Alister: A variant of 'Alexander', meaning 'defending man'.

Allan: A variant of 'Alan', meaning 'in tune'.

Allarde: From this surname, from 'Picardy' in France, meaning 'brave and noble'.

Allen: A variant of 'Alan', meaning 'in tune'.

Allyn: A variant of 'Alan', meaning 'in tune'.

Almar: A name mentioned in the Domesday book of the 11th century, and from the Anglo Saxon, meaning 'noble' ('Aethelmar').

Almaric: From the Anglo Saxon 'Aethelmar', and meaning 'noble'. This name is mentioned in records in Berkshire in the 13th century.

Almeric: From the Teutonic, meaning 'energetic'.

Alnod: The name of a landholder mentioned in the Domesday book of A.D. 1087. Little used today.

Alonso: Spanish for 'Alphonso', and meaning a 'ready noble'.

Alonzo: A variant of 'Alphonso', and meaning a 'ready noble'.

Aloysius and **Aloisius:** From the Latin, meaning a 'warrior'. St. Aloysius lived in Italy in the 16th century.

Alphonse: French for 'Alphonso', and meaning a 'ready noble'.

Alphonso: From the Teutonic, and meaning a 'ready noble'. A variant is *Alfonso*.

Alric: Little used as a Christian name today but the name of a bishop mentioned in the Domesday book of A.D. 1087. Possibly from the Germanic 'Almaric', meaning an 'energetic ruler' and 'noble'.

Alston: From the Anglo Saxon 'Aethelston', and meaning 'of noble estate'.

Alun: A variant of 'Alan', and meaning 'in tune'.

Aluric: A name mentioned in the Domesday book of the 11th century, and meaning 'elf's counsel'.

Alva: From the Latin, meaning 'blond'. Examples: *Alva Edison*.

Alvin: From the Old German 'Alh-win', meaning 'great friend'.

Alvis: From the Norse 'Alviss', meaning 'full of wisdom'.

Alvred: A name which is recorded in the Domesday book and is the same name as 'Alfred', meaning 'elf's counsel'. Little used today.

Alwin: From the Anglo Saxon 'Aethelwin', and meaning 'friendly'. This name is mentioned in the Domesday book of A.D. 1087.

Alwyn: From the Anglo Saxon 'Aethelwin', meaning 'friendly'.

Amadeus: From the Latin, meaning 'Lover of God'. Example: *Wolfgang Amadeus Mozart*.

Ambroise: French for 'Ambrose', meaning 'immortal'.

Ambrose: From the Greek 'Ambrosio', meaning 'immortal'.

Ambrosi: Italian for 'Ambrose', meaning 'immortal'.

Ambrosio: Spanish for 'Ambrose', meaning 'immortal'.

Ambrosius: Dutch and Swedish for 'Ambrose', meaning 'immortal'.

Amerigo: Italian for 'Emery', meaning a 'ruler'. Example: *Amerigo Vespucci*.

Amery: From the old German, meaning a 'noted ruler'.

Amory: From the old German 'Almaric', meaning a 'noted ruler'.

Amos: From the Hebrew, meaning 'bearer of a burden'. Amos was a prophet mentioned in the Bible.

Amyas: From this surname, and meaning 'coming from Amiens'. Also Amias.

Anastasius: From the Greek, meaning 'risen again'.

Anatole: From the Greek, meaning a 'man from the east'. Example: *Anatole France*.

Anatolio: Spanish for 'Anatole', and meaning 'man from the east'.

Anders: Swedish for 'Andrew', meaning 'manly'.

André: This is French for 'Andrew', meaning 'manly'. Examples: *André Ampere, André Gide.*

Andrea: Italian for 'Andrew', meaning 'manly'.

Audreas: Dutch and Swedish for 'Andrew', meaning 'manly'.

Andres: Spanish for 'Andrew', meaning 'manly'.

Andrew: From the Greek, meaning 'manly'. A variant is *Andy.* Example: *Andrew Jackson.* St. Andrew is the Patron Saint of Scotland.

Aneurin: Welsh, meaning 'truly golden'.

Angelo: From the Italian, meaning 'angel'.

Angus: From the Gaelic, meaning 'unique choice'.

Anselm: From the Teutonic, meaning 'divine helmet'.

Anselme: French for 'Anselm', meaning 'divine helmet'.

Anselmi: Italian for 'Anselm', and meaning 'divine helmet'.

Anselmo: Portuguese and Spanish for 'Anselm', and meaning 'divine helmet'.

Ansfrid: A Norman name which is little used today, but it was the name of a landowner in the Domesday book of the 11th century.

Anthony: From the Latin 'Antonius', meaning 'strong'. A variant is *Tony.* St. Anthony of Padua lived in the 13th century.

Anton: Swedish and German for 'Anthony', meaning 'strong'.

Antonio: Italian, Spanish and Portuguese for 'Anthony', meaning 'strong'.

Antony: From the Latin, meaning 'strong'.

Araldo: Italian for 'Harold', meaning 'army chief'.

Archambault: French for 'Archibald', and meaning 'sacred and bold'.

Archibald: Means 'sacred and bold'.

Archimbald: German for 'Archibald', and meaning 'sacred and bold'.

Aristide: From the French, meaning the 'best son'.

Armand: French for 'Herman', meaning 'warrior'.

Armando: Spanish for 'Herman', meaning 'warrior'.

Armitage: From this surname, and meaning 'one who lived by the hermitage'.

Arnaldo: Spanish for 'Arnold', meaning 'with the power of an eagle'.

Arnaud: French for 'Arnold', meaning 'with the power of an eagle'.

Arnold: Meaning 'with the power of an eagle'. Example: *Arnold Bennett.*

Arnoldo: Italian for 'Arnold', meaning 'with the power of an eagle'.

Art: A diminutive of 'Arthur', meaning 'eagle of Thor'.

Arthur: From the Norse, meaning 'eagle of Thor'. A variant is *Art.* Example: *King Arthur.*

Arturo: Italian and Spanish for 'Arthur', meaning 'eagle of Thor'.

Artus: French for 'Arthur', meaning 'eagle of Thor'.

Asa: From the Hebrew, meaning 'physician'.

Asher: From the Hebrew, meaning 'fortunate'. In the Bible, Asher was the son of Jacob (Genesis 30.13).

Athold: From the Scottish family of the 'Dukes of Atholl', and the place of this name.

Aubert: French for 'Albert', meaning 'bright and noble'.

Aubin: French for 'Albin', meaning 'one who is fair'.

Aubrey: From the Teutonic 'Albertic', meaning 'blond ruler'.

Augustine: Means 'belonging to Augustus'. St. Augustine was the first Archbishop of Canterbury.

Augustus: Meaning 'majestic'. Variants are *Gus* and *Gussy.* Example: *Augustus John.*

Austen: A variant of 'Augustine', meaning 'belonging to Augustus'.

Austin: A variant of 'Augustine', meaning 'belonging to Augustus'.

Aveary: A variant of 'Avery', meaning a 'ruler of elves'.

Avery: Meaning a 'ruler of elves'.

Avison: Meaning a 'son of Avice or Avicia'.

Aylmer: From the Teutonic, meaning 'famous noble'.

Aylward: From the old English 'Agilward', meaning a 'guardian'.

Aylwyn: From the old English 'Aethelwin', meaning a 'noble friend'.

Baldovin: Italian for 'Baldwin', meaning 'bold friend'.

Baldwin: From the Germanic 'Baldavin', meaning 'bold friend'. This name is mentioned in the Domesday book (11th century). Baldwin was the Count of Flanders in the 9th century.

Balthasar: From the Semitic, meaning the 'king's protector'. This was the name of one of the Three Wise Men.

Barclay: From this surname, meaning 'one who lived by the birch meadow'.

Barnaba: Italian for 'Barnabas', meaning 'son of exhortation'.

Barnabas: From the Hebrew, meaning 'son of exhortation' (Acts 11.22). Variants are *Barney*, *Barnaby*. Example: *Barnaby Rudge.*

Barnabe: French for 'Barnabas', meaning 'son of exhortation'.

Barnaby: A variant of 'Barnabas', meaning 'son of exhortation'.

Barnard: French for 'Bernard', meaning 'brave as a bear'.

Barnebas: Spanish for 'Barnabas', meaning 'son of exhortation'.

Barnett: A variant of 'Bernard', meaning 'brave as a bear'.

Baron: From the old English, meaning 'noble'.

Barrie: From the Celtic 'Bearach', meaning 'spearman'.

Barry: From the Celtic 'Bearach', meaning 'spearman'.

Bart: A diminutive of 'Bartholomew', meaning 'son of Talmai'.

Barthel: German for 'Bartholomew', meaning 'son of Talmai'.

Barthelemy: French for 'Bartholomew', meaning 'son of Talmai'.

Bartholomeus: Dutch and Swedish for 'Bartholomew', meaning 'son of Talmai'.

Bartholomew: Semitic, and meaning 'son of Talmai'. Variants are *Bat*, *Bart* and *Barty*.

Barthram: From the Teutonic, meaning 'bright raven'. A variant is *Bart*.

Bartimaeus: Means the 'son of Timaeus' (Mark 10.46). A variant is *Bart*.

Bartlemy: A variant of 'Bartholomew', meaning 'son of Talmai'.

Bartolome: Spanish for 'Bartholomew', meaning 'son of Talmai'.

Bartolomeo: Italian for 'Bartholomew', meaning 'son of Talmai'.

Bartram: From the Teutonic 'Beorhtram', meaning the 'bright raven'.

Basil: From the Greek 'Basileios', meaning 'royal'.

Basile: French for 'Basil', meaning 'royal'.

Basilio: Spanish and Italian for 'Basil', meaning 'royal'.

Basilius: Dutch and Swedish for 'Basil', meaning 'royal'.

Bassett: From the French 'Le bas', meaning 'small in stature'.

Baudoin: French for 'Baldwin', meaning 'bold friend'.

Baxter: From this surname, meaning a 'baker'.

Beau: From the French 'Beau', meaning 'handsome'. Examples: *Beau Geste* and *Beau Nash*.

Beltran: Spanish for 'Bertram', meaning 'bright raven'.

Ben: A diminutive of 'Benedict' and 'Benjamin'.

Benedetto: Italian for 'Benedict', meaning 'blessed'.

Benedict: From the Latin 'Benedictus', meaning 'blessed'. Benedict was a 5th century saint.

Bengt: Swedish for 'Benedict', meaning 'blessed'.

Benito: Spanish and Italian for 'Benedict', meaning 'blessed'.

Benjamin: From the Hebrew, meaning 'son of my right hand' (Genesis 35.18). Variants are *Ben*, *Benny* and *Benjie*. Examples: *Benjamin Franklin* and *Benjamin Disraeli*.

Benjamino: Italian for 'Benjamin', meaning 'son of my right hand'.

Benjie: A variant of 'Benjamin', meaning 'son of my right hand'.

Benny: A variant of 'Benjamin', meaning 'son of my right hand'.

Benoit: French for 'Benedict', meaning 'blessed'.

Bernard: From the German, meaning 'brave as a bear'. Variants are *Bern* and *Bernie*. Example: *Bernard Shaw*.

Bernardo: Spanish and Italian for 'Bernard', meaning 'brave as a bear'.

Bernhard: Swedish and German for 'Bernard', meaning 'brave as a bear'.

Bert: A diminutive of 'Albert' and 'Bertram'.

Bertram: From the Teutonic, meaning 'bright raven'. Variants are *Bert* and *Bertie*.

Bertrand: French for 'Bertram'. Example: *Bertrand Russell*.

Beverley: From this surname, meaning 'one who dwells by the beaver meadow'.

Bevis: From the old French, meaning a 'bull'.

Bill and **Billy:** A variant of 'William'.

Bing: From the old German, meaning 'from the hollow'.

Blake: From the old English, meaning a 'dark one'.

Blakeley: From this surname, and meaning 'one who dwells by the black meadow'.

Boaz: From the Hebrew 'Boaz', meaning 'in the Lord's strength'.

Bonar: From the old French, meaning 'gentle'.

Boniface: From the Latin, meaning a 'good man'.

Bonifacio: Spanish and Italian for 'Boniface', meaning a 'good man'.

Bonifacius: Dutch, Swedish and German for 'Boniface', meaning a 'good man'.

Boris: From the Russian, and meaning a 'fighter'.

Boyd: From the Gaelic, meaning 'blond'.

Boyle: Means 'born in the time of danger'.

Bracy: From the surname 'Brescie', and a name mentioned in the Rolls of Battle Abbey A.D. 1066.

Brad: A diminutive of 'Bradley'.

Bradley: From this surname, and meaning 'one who lives by the broad meadow'.

Bram: A variant of 'Abraham', meaning 'father of the people'.

Bramwell: From the old English, meaning 'from the bramble spring'.

Brendan: From the Irish, meaning 'a dweller on the hill'.

Bret: Meaning a 'Briton'.

Brewster: From this surname, and meaning a 'brewer'.

Brian: From the Celtic, and meaning 'strong'.

Briano: Italian for 'Brian', meaning 'strong'.

Briant: From the Celtic, meaning 'strong'.

Brice: From the Welsh 'Brys', meaning a 'fast one'.

Brigham: From the old English, meaning 'dweller by the bridge'.

Brindley: From the Anglo Saxon, meaning 'one who lives on the brow of the hill'.

Brinton: Meaning 'one who lives by the burnt town'. This name is mentioned in the records at Somerset House in 1901.

Broderick: From the German, meaning 'son of the ruler'.

Bruce: From the French place of 'Bruis', and this surname.

Bruno: From the Italian, and meaning 'one with brown hair'.

Bryan: From the Celtic, meaning 'strong'.

Bryant: From the Celtic, meaning 'strong'.

Bryce: An English variant of 'Brice'.

Bryn: A Welsh Christian name, meaning a 'hill'.

Burl: From the old English, meaning 'cup bearer'.

Caesar: From the Latin, meaning 'longhaired', and later 'emperor'. Example: *Caesar Borgia*.

Cain: Means 'possessed' and comes from the biblical name, and the French town of 'Caen'. Not a popular Christian name because of Cain's murder of his brother Abel.

Calder: From this surname and from the Gaelic, meaning 'one who lived by the oak wood'.

Caleb: From the Hebrew, meaning 'faithful', mentioned in Numbers 13.30.

Caley: From the Irish Gaelic, meaning 'slender'.

Calhoun: From the Irish surname, and meaning 'from the forest'.

Calvert: From this surname, and meaning 'of the green'. A variant is *Cal*.

Calvin: From the Latin, and meaning 'bald'.

Calvino: Spanish and Italian for 'Calvin', meaning 'bald'.

Campbell: From this surname, and meaning 'one who has a crooked mouth'.

Canute: From the Norse, and meaning a 'knot'. Example: *King Canute*.

Caradoc: From the Celtic, meaning 'beloved'.

Carey: From this Welsh surname, and meaning 'castle dweller'.

Carl: From the German 'Karl', meaning 'strong'. Swedish and German for 'Charles'.

Carleton: From the surname 'Carlton', meaning 'from the farmer's place'.

Carlisle: From this surname, and meaning 'of the castle tower'.

Carlo: Italian for 'Charles', meaning 'strong'.

Carlos: Spanish for 'Charles', meaning 'strong'.

Carmichael: From the Gaelic, meaning 'loved of St. Michael'.

Carol: From 'Carolus' (the Latin for 'Charles'), meaning 'strong'.

Carr: From this surname, and meaning a 'marsh dweller'.

Carson: From this surname, meaning 'son of a marsh dweller'.

Carter: From this surname, and meaning a 'driver'.

Carthew: From the Cornish, meaning 'a rock or large stone'.

Carver: From the Cornish 'Car-veor', meaning 'great rock'. Example: *Carver Doone*.

Cary: From the old Welsh, meaning 'castle dweller'.

Cäsar: German for 'Caesar', meaning 'longhaired', and later 'emperor'.

Casey: Irish for 'brave'.

Cashel: A name given to a boy who was born in this part of Ireland.

Caspar: From the Persian, meaning 'master of the treasure'.

Cassidy: From this Irish surname, meaning 'clever'.

Cavan: From the Irish Gaelic, meaning 'handsome'.

Cecil: From the Latin, meaning the 'blind one'. Example: *Cecil Rhodes*.

Cécile: French for 'Cecil', and meaning the 'blind one'.

Cecilius: Dutch for 'Cecil', and meaning the 'blind one'.

Cedric: From the Celtic, meaning 'bountiful'.

César: French and Spanish for 'Caesar', meaning 'emperor'.

Cesare: Italian for 'Caesar', meaning 'emperor'.

Chad: From the old English, meaning 'warlike'.

Charles: From the German 'Karl', meaning a 'man'. Variants are *Chas* and *Charlie*. Example: *Charles Dickens*.

Charlton: From this surname, meaning 'peasant's place'.

Chester: From the old English 'Caester', meaning 'camp dweller'.

Chrétien: French for 'Christian', meaning a 'believer'.

Chris: A diminutive of 'Christopher'.

Christian: From the Greek, meaning a 'believer'. A variant is *Chris*.

Christiano: Spanish and Italian for 'Christian', meaning a 'believer'.

Christie: A variant of 'Christopher', meaning 'Christ's bearer'.

Christmas: Usually given to one born at Christmas. A variant is *Chris*.

Christoffer: Danish for 'Christopher', meaning 'Christ's bearer'.

Christophe: French for 'Christopher', meaning 'Christ's bearer'.

Christopher: From the Greek, meaning 'Christ's bearer'. Variants are Kit and Chris. Example: *Christopher Columbus*.

Christophorus: German for 'Christopher', meaning 'Christ's bearer'.

Chuck: A variant of 'Charles', meaning a 'man'.

Cipriano: Spanish for 'Cyprian', meaning a 'native of Cyprus'.

Cirillo: Italian for 'Cyril', meaning 'lordly'.

Cirilo: Spanish for 'Cyril', meaning 'lordly'.

Ciro: Spanish for 'Cyrus', meaning 'of the throne'.

Clarence: From the Latin, meaning 'famous one'.

Claridge: Means the 'son of Clarice'.

Clark: Means 'one who is learned'.

Clarry: A variant of 'Clarence', meaning 'famous'.

Clarus: From the Latin. Clarus meaning 'famous'.

Claude: From the Latin, meaning 'lame'.

Claudio: Spanish and Italian for 'Claude', meaning 'lame'.

Claudius: Dutch and German for 'Claude', meaning 'lame'.

Claus: A variant of 'Nicholas', meaning 'victorious'.

Clegg: From the Cornish, meaning a 'rock'.

Clem: A diminutive of 'Clement'.

Clemens: Danish for 'Clement', meaning 'merciful'.

Clement: From the Latin, meaning 'merciful'. A variant is Clem.

Clemente: Spanish and Italian for 'Clement', meaning 'merciful'.

Clementius: Dutch for 'Clement', meaning 'merciful'.

Cliff: Means 'one who lived by the cliff'.

Clifford: From this surname, and means 'one who lived by the cliff ford'. A variant is *Cliff*.

Clift: Means 'one who lived by the cliff'.

Clifton: Means 'one who lived by the town cliff'. A variant is *Cliff*.

Clint and **Clinton:** From the old English, meaning 'from the headland'.

Clive: From this surname, and means 'one who lived by the cliff'.

Clovis: From the old German, meaning 'warrior'.

Colbert: From the German, meaning 'bright one'.

Colin: From 'Nicholas', meaning 'victorious'.

Conan: From the Gaelic, meaning 'high exalted'. Example: *Sir A. Conan Doyle*.

Connel: From the Gaelic, meaning 'courageous'.

Connor: From the Gaelic, meaning 'courageous'.

Conrad: From the German, meaning a 'bold counsellor'.

Conrade: French for 'Conrad', meaning a 'bold counsellor'.

Conrado: Spanish and Italian for 'Conrad', meaning a 'bold counsellor'.

Constantin: French, German and Dutch for 'Constantine', and meaning 'constant'.

Constantine: From the Latin, meaning 'constant'.

Constantino: Spanish and Italian for 'Constantine', meaning 'constant'.

Cornelio: Spanish and Italian for 'Cornelius', meaning 'horn like'.

Cornelius: From the Latin, meaning 'horn like'.

Cosimo: Spanish and Italian for 'Cosmo', meaning 'world harmony'.

Cosme: French for 'Cosmo', meaning 'world harmony'.

Cosmo: From the Greek, meaning 'world harmony'.

Courtney: From this surname, and meaning a 'courtier'.

Craig: From the Scots Gaelic, meaning 'dweller at a crag'.

Crépin: French for 'Crispin', meaning 'curly haired'.

Crispin: From the Latin, meaning 'curly haired'. St. Crispin was the Patron Saint of Shoemakers.

Crispino: Italian for 'Crispin', meaning 'curly haired'.

Crispo: Spanish for 'Crispin', meaning 'curly haired'.

Crispus: German for 'Crispin', meaning 'curly haired'.

Christobal: Spanish for 'Christopher', meaning 'Christ's bearer'.

Christoforo: Italian for 'Christopher', meaning 'Christ's bearer'.

Curtis: From the French, and meaning 'courteous'.

Cuthbert: From the Anglo Saxon 'Cuthbeort', and meaning 'bright'.

Cyprian: Means a 'native of Cyprus'.

Cyril: From the Greek, meaning 'lordly'.

Cyrill: German for 'Cyril', meaning 'lordly'.

Cyrille: French for 'Cyril', meaning 'lordly'.

Cyrillus: Swedish, Dutch and Danish for 'Cyril', meaning 'lordly'.

Cyrus: From the Persian, meaning 'of the throne'.

Dagmar: From the Teutonic, meaning 'bright day'.

Dai: From the Welsh, meaning 'fiery'.

Damian: French for 'Damon'.

Damiano: Italian for 'Damon'.

Damien: From the Greek, meaning 'to tame'.

Damon: From the Greek, meaning 'conqueror'.

Dan: A diminutive of 'Daniel'.

Dandie: The name sometimes given to boys in Scotland named 'Andrew'.

Dane: Dutch for 'Daniel', and also meaning 'one who comes from Denmark'.

Daniel: From the Hebrew, meaning 'God is my judge' (Daniel 1.6). Daniel was a son of Jacob (Genesis 30.6). Variants are *Dan* and *Danny*. Example: *Daniel Defoe.*

Danielle: Italian for 'Daniel'.

Danny: A variant of 'Daniel'.

Darby: From the Gaelic, meaning a 'freeman'. Example: *Darby and Joan.*

D'arcy and Darcy: From the French surname, and 'Arci' (a place in Normandy). Mention is made of this name in the Battle Abbey Rolls of A.D. 1066.

Darius: From the Persian, meaning a 'good man'. Darius was a king of Persia.

Darrell: From this surname, and from 'D'Arel' in Normandy. Mentioned in the Battle Abbey Rolls of A.D. 1066.

Darren: From the Gaelic, meaning 'little one'. Also 'Darran'.

Darroch: A Scottish Christian name, meaning 'strong as an oak'.

Daryl: From the French, meaning 'one beloved'.

David: From the Hebrew, meaning 'beloved'. Variants are *Dave, Davy* and *Davie*. Example: *David Livingstone.*

Davidde: Italian for 'David'.

Davide: French for 'David'.

Dean: From the old English surname, and the name often given to one who dwelt in a 'valley' or 'dene'.

Decimus: From the Latin, meaning the 'tenth'. Example: *Decimus Burton.*

Demetre: French for 'Demetrius'.

Demetrio: Italian for 'Demetrius'.

Demetrius: From the Greek goddess of the harvest, i.e. 'Demeter', and meaning 'belonging to Demeter'. Demetrius was a silversmith in the Bible.

Dennis and **Denis:** From 'Dionysius', the Greek god of wine. A variant is *Denny.*

Denzil: From the Celtic, meaning 'stronghold'.

Derek and **Derrick:** From the German 'Theodoric', meaning 'ruler of the people'. Variants are *Dirk* and *Derry.*

Dermot: From the Irish 'Diamid', meaning a 'free man'.

Derry: A variant of 'Derek'.

Desmond: From the Irish clan name, meaning a 'man of South Munster'.

Dexter: From the Latin, meaning 'skilful'.

Dick: A variant of 'Richard'.

Digby: From this surname, and meaning 'one who lived by the dyke'.

Dingle: An old English Christian name but little used today. Possibly from the Anglo Saxon 'Dingolf'.

Dionisio: Spanish and Italian for 'Dennis'.

Dionysus: German for 'Dennis'.

Dirk: A variant of 'Derrick'.

Dmitri: Russian for 'Demetrius'.

Domenico: Italian for 'Dominic'.

Domingo: Spanish for 'Dominic'.

Dominic: From the Latin, meaning 'of the Lord'.

Dominique: French for 'Dominic'.

Dominy: A variant of 'Dominic'.

Donald: From the Gaelic, meaning 'world ruler'. A variant is *Don*.

Dorian: From the Greek, meaning 'one who came from the ancient Greek place named Doria'. Example: *Dorian Gray*.

Dougal: A Scottish form of 'Douglas'.

Douglas: From the Gaelic 'Dubhglas', meaning 'of the black water'. Variants are *Doug* and *Duggie*.

D'oyley: From 'Ouilly' in Falaise in France. Mentioned in the Rolls of Battle Abbey in A.D. 1066. Example: *D'oyley Carte*.

Drew: From the German, meaning 'trustworthy'.

Dudley: From this surname, meaning 'of the meadow of Duda'.

Duffy: From the Irish 'Duff', meaning 'dark skinned'.

Dugald: From the Gaelic, meaning a 'dark stranger'.

Duggie: A variant of 'Douglas'.

Duguid: A Scottish Christian name, meaning 'one who does good'.

Duke: From the French 'Duc', meaning 'leader'.

Duncan: A Scottish name, meaning 'black haired'.

Dunstan: From the old English, meaning 'of the brown stone'. Example: *St. Dunstan*.

Durand: An uncommon Christian name today but one which is mentioned as a landholder in the Domesday book (11th century).

Dwight: Means 'white haired'.

Dylan: From the Welsh, meaning 'up from the sea'.

Eachan: From the Gaelic, meaning a 'horse'.

Eamonn: Irish for 'Edmund'.

Earl: From the Anglo Saxon 'Eorl', meaning a 'nobleman'. Mostly used in U.S.A. today. Variants are *Erle* and *Earle*.

Ebenezer: From the Hebrew, meaning 'stone of help'. Variants are *Eb* and *Ebbie*.

Edbert: From the old English, meaning 'bright'.

Eddie: Variant of 'Edward', 'Edmund', 'Edwin' and 'Edgar'.

Eden: From the Hebrew, meaning a 'pleasant place'.

Edgar: From the Anglo Saxon 'Eadgar', meaning 'spear of prosperity'. Variants are *Eddie* and *Ed*.

Edgard: French for 'Edgar'.

Edgardo: Italian for 'Edgar'.

Edmar: Mentioned in the Domesday book (11th century) but little used now.

Edmond: Dutch and French for 'Edmund'.

Edmund: From the Anglo Saxon 'Eadmund', meaning 'spear of riches'. Variants are *Ed* and *Eddie*. Example: *Edmund Spencer*.

Edmundo: Spanish for 'Edmund'.

Edouardo: French for 'Edward'.

Edric: From the Anglo Saxon, meaning a 'wealthy ruler'.

Edsel: From the Anglo Saxon, meaning 'wealthy giver'.

Eduard: Dutch and German for 'Edward'.

Eduardo: Spanish and Italian for 'Edward'.

Eduino: Italian for 'Edwin'.

Edvard: Danish and Swedish for 'Edward'.

Edward: From the Anglo Saxon, meaning 'wealthy guardian'. Edward was the name of a landowner mentioned in the Domesday book in the 11th century. Variants are *Ted, Ed* and *Eddie*. Examples: *Edward the Confessor, Edward Lear* and *Sir Edward Elgar*.

Edwin: From the Anglo Saxon 'Eadwine', meaning 'prosperous friend'. Variants are *Ed* and *Eddie*.

Egbert: From the Anglo Saxon 'Egbeorht', meaning 'shining sword'.

Egidio: Italian for 'Giles'.

Egmond: As 'Egmont .

Egmont: From the Anglo Saxon, meaning 'sword's protection'.

Elbert: A variant of 'Albert'. Example: *Elbert Hubbard*.

Eli: A diminutive of 'Elias' and 'Elijah'. From the Hebrew, meaning 'high'. Eli was a high priest in the Old Testament.

Elia: Italian for 'Elijah'.

Elias: Dutch and German for 'Elijah'. Example: *Elias Howe*.

Elie: French for 'Elijah'.

Elijah: From the Hebrew, meaning 'Jehovah is God'. Elijah was a prophet in the Old Testament.

Eliot: As for 'Elliot'.

Elisee: French for 'Elisha'.

Eliseo: Spanish and Italian for 'Elisha'.

Elisha: Meaning 'God is my salvation'. Elisha was a prophet in the Old Testament (1 Kings 19.16).

Ellery: From the Middle English meaning 'From the elder tree'.

Elliot: A variant of 'Ellis' and 'Elijah' meaning 'Jehovah is God'.

Ellis: A variant of 'Elijah'.

Elmer: From the Anglo Saxon 'Aethelmaer', meaning 'famous nobel'. This is used as a Christian name in U.S.A.

Elmo: From the Greek, meaning 'amiable'.

Elroy: From 'Le roi', meaning 'the king'.

Elvin: As 'Elwin'.

Elvis: From the Norse, meaning 'wise one'.

Elwin: From the Anglo Saxon, meaning 'friend of the elf'.

Ely: As 'Eli'.

Emeri: French for 'Emery'.

Emery: From the Teutonic 'Amalric', meaning a 'great ruler'.

Emil: From the Teutonic, meaning 'industrious'.

Emile: French for 'Emil'. Example: *Emile Zola.*

Emilio: Spanish for 'Emil'.

Emlyn: From the Welsh, meaning 'lordly'.

Emmanuel: From the Hebrew, meaning 'God with us' (Isaiah 7.14). A variant is *Manny.*

Emmanuele: Italian for 'Emmanuel'.

Emmerich: German for 'Emery'.

Emmett: From the Teutonic, meaning 'industrious'.

Emmot: As 'Emmett'.

Emory: As 'Emery'.

Eneas: From the Greek, meaning 'one to be praised'. Spanish for 'Aeneas'.

Engelbert: From the Teutonic, meaning a 'bright angel'.

Enne: French for 'Aeneas'.

Ennis: From the Gaelic, meaning the 'chief one'.

Enoch: From the Hebrew, meaning 'consecrated'. In the Bible, Enoch was the father of Methuselah.

Enrico: Italian for 'Henry'.

Enrique: Spanish for 'Henry'.

Ephraim: From the Hebrew, meaning 'fruitful'. Ephraim was the son of Joseph (Genesis 41.52).

Erasme: French for 'Erasmus'.

Erasmo: Spanish and Italian for 'Erasmus'.

Erasmus: From the Greek, meaning 'beloved'.

Eraste: French for 'Erastus'.

Erastus: From the Greek, meaning 'beloved'. Mentioned in Acts 19.22. Variants are *Ras* and *Rastus*.

Eric: From the Norse, meaning 'ruler'. Variants are *Rick* and *Ricky*.

Ermin: A Welsh name, meaning 'lordly'.

Ernald: Mentioned in the Domesday book (11th century). A variant of 'Arnold'.

Ernest: From the Anglo Saxon, meaning 'earnest'. Variants are *Ern* and *Ernie*.

Ernesto: Spanish and Italian for 'Ernest'.

Ernestus: Dutch for 'Ernest'.

Ernst: German for 'Ernest'.

Errol: From the Anglo Saxon 'Eorl', meaning 'noble'. A Scottish variant of 'Earl'.

Erwin: From the Anglo Saxon 'Eoforwine', meaning the 'sea's friend'.

Esau: From the Hebrew, meaning 'hairy'. Esau was the son of Jacob (Genesis 25.25).

Esme: From the Latin, meaning 'esteemed'.

Esmond: From the Teutonic, meaning 'divine protector'.

Esteban: Spanish for 'Stephen'.

Ethelbert: From the Anglo Saxon, meaning 'bright and noble'.

Ethelred: From the Anglo Saxon, meaning 'bright and noble'.

Etienne: French for 'Stephen'.

Ettore: Italian for 'Hector'.

Eugen: German for 'Eugene'.

Eugene: From the Greek, meaning 'nobly born'.

Eugenio: Spanish and Italian for 'Eugene'.

Eugenius: Dutch for 'Eugene'.

Euraud: French for 'Everard'.

Eusebius: From the Greek, meaning 'reverent'.

Eustace: From the Greek, meaning 'good harvest'.

Eustache: French for 'Eustace'.

Eustasius: German for 'Eustace'.

Eustatius: Dutch for 'Eustace'.

Eustazio: Italian for 'Eustace'.

Eustquio: Spanish for 'Eustace'.

Evan: From the Welsh, meaning 'warrior'.

Evelyn: From the French, meaning 'hazel'.

Everard: From the Teutonic, meaning 'with the strength of a boar'.

Everardo: Italian for 'Everard'.

Everhart: Dutch for 'Everard'.

Everley: From this surname, and meaning 'one who dwelt in the boar meadow'.

Ewan: From the Gaelic, meaning a 'warrior'.

Ewart: From this surname, and meaning 'with the strength of a boar'. Scottish form of 'Everard'. Example: *W. Ewart Gladstone*.

Ewing: A Scottish name, meaning 'fiery'.

Eylmer: A name mentioned in the Assize Rolls (13th century) as 'Aylmer'.

Ezequiel: Spanish for 'Ezekiel'.

Ezra: From the Hebrew, meaning 'help'. Example: *Ezra Read*.

Fabian: From the Latin 'Faba', meaning a 'bean grower'.

Fabiano: Italian for 'Fabian'.

Fabien: French for 'Fabian'.

Fancourt: From 'Fovecourt', near Beauvais, France.

Fane: From the surname, meaning 'joyful'.

Farrell: From the Gaelic, meaning a 'warrior'.

Federico: Spanish for 'Frederick'.

Federigo: Italian for 'Frederick'.

Felice: Italian for 'Felix'.

Felipe: Spanish for 'Philip'.

Felix: From the Latin, meaning 'lucky'.

Ferdinand: From the Teutonic, meaning 'bold peace'. A variant is *Ferdie*.

Fergie: As 'Fergus'.

Fergus: From the Celtic, meaning 'man of strength'.

Ferrers and **Ferrier:** From the Norman family name of 'Ferrieres'.

Fidel: From the Latin 'Fidelis', meaning 'faithful'.

Fidele: French for 'Fidel'.

Fidelio: Italian for 'Fidel'.

Filip: Swedish for 'Philip'.

Filippo: Italian for 'Philip'.

Findlay: From the Gaelic, meaning 'fair haired'.

Fingal: From the Celtic, meaning a 'white stranger'. Example: *Fingal's Cave.*

Finlay: A Scottish name, meaning 'light haired'.

Fleming: A Scottish name, meaning a 'refugee'.

Fletcher: From this surname, meaning an 'arrowmaker'. Example: *Fletcher Christian.*

Flint: From the Anglo Saxon, meaning 'brook'.

Floyd: From the Welsh, meaning 'grey haired'.

Forbes: From the Gaelic, meaning 'prosperous'.

Ford: From this surname, and meaning 'one who lived at the ford'.

Fordyce: A Scottish name, meaning 'man of wisdom'.

Forrest: From this surname, meaning 'one who dwells in the forest'.

Foster: From the same surname as 'Forrester', meaning 'one who looked after the forest'.

Francesco: Italian for Francis'.

Franchot: French for 'Francis'.

Francis: From the Latin 'Franciscus', meaning a 'freeman'. Example: *Francis Bacon.*

Francisco: Spanish for 'Francis'.

François: French for 'Francis'.

Frane: A name meaning a 'foreigner'. Mentioned in the Domesday book.

Frank: From the Teutonic, meaning 'free'.

Franklin: From the Anglo Saxon, meaning a 'freeholder'. A variant is *Frank*.

Frans: Swedish for 'Francis'.

Frants: Danish for 'Francis'.

Franz: German for 'Francis'.

Fraser: A Scottish name, meaning a 'planter of strawberries'.

Frederic: French for 'Frederick'.

Frederick: From the Teutonic, meaning a 'peaceful ruler'. Variants are *Fred* and *Freddie*. Example: *Frederick the Great*.

Fredrik: Swedish for 'Frederick'.

Freeman: From the Anglo Saxon, meaning a 'freeholder'.

Fritz: A German variant of 'Frederick'.

Fulk: From the Norman 'Folkard', meaning the 'strong people'.

Fyfe: A 'native of Fife'.

Gabby: A variant of 'Gabriel'.

Gabriel: From the Hebrew, meaning 'man of God'. Variants are *Gab* and *Gabby*. Examples: *The Archangel Gabriel* (Daniel 8.16), *Gabriel Rossetti*.

Gabriello: Italian for 'Gabriel'.

Gad: From the Hebrew, meaning 'good fortune'.

Gale: From the Anglo Saxon, meaning 'gay'.

Galloway: Scottish, and meaning a 'man from Galloway'.

Gareth: Meaning 'one who ravages'.

Garfield: From this surname, and meaning 'one who lives by the battlefield'.

Garnet: From the stone 'Garnet'.

Garrard: From the name 'Gerard'.

Garreth: From the name 'Gerard'.

Garth: From the Teutonic, meaning 'one who ravages'.

Gary: From the Anglo Saxon, meaning a 'spear'.

Gaspar: From the Persian, meaning 'master of the treasures'. Variants are *Caspar* and *Jasper*. Gaspar was the name of one of the Magi in the Bible.

Gaspard: French for 'Gaspar'.

Gasparo: Italian for 'Gaspar'.

Gaston: From the French, and meaning a 'man of Gascony'.

Gavin: From the Celtic, and meaning 'hawk man'.

Gawain: From the Celtic, and meaning 'hawk man'. Gawain was one of the knights of King Arthur.

Gaylord: From the French 'Gaillard', meaning 'brisk'.

Gaynor: Meaning 'son of the fair head'.

Gedeon: The Greek form of 'Gideon'.

Geoffrey: From the German, meaning 'peace of God'. A variant is *Jeffrey*.

Georg: Danish, German and Swedish for 'George'.

Georgdie: A North of England and Scottish variant of 'George'.

George: From the Greek, meaning a 'farmer'. A variant is *Georgie*. Example: *George Washington*.

Georges: French for 'George'.

Geraint: From the Celtic, meaning 'ruler with a spear'. Geraint was the name of a Cornish saint.

Gerald: From the Teutonic, meaning 'ruler with a spear'. A variant is *Gerry*.

Gerard: From the Teutonic, meaning 'ruler with a spear'.

Gerardo: Italian for 'Gerard'.

Gerhard: Swedish and Danish for 'Gerard'.

Gerhardt: German for 'Gerard'.

Gerold: A variant of 'Gerald', mentioned in the Domesday book (11th century).

Gervase: Means 'spearman'. Gervase was the name of a monk in the Middle Ages. Example: *Gervase of Canterbury*.

Giacomo: Italian for 'Jacob'.

Gibson: From this surname, and meaning the 'son of Gilbert'.

Gideon: From the Hebrew, and meaning 'one who cuts down'.

Gifford: From the Anglo Saxon, meaning 'brave gift'. A variant is *Giff*.

Gil: Spanish for 'Giles'.

Gilbert: From the Teutonic, meaning a 'bright hostage'. A variant is *Gil*.

Gilberto: Italian for 'Gilbert'.

Gilbey: From the Teutonic, meaning 'by a pledge'.

Gilchrist: From the Gaelic, meaning a 'servant of Christ'.

Giles: From the French, meaning 'youthful'.

Gilles: As 'Gillespie'.

Gillespie: From this Celtic surname, meaning 'bishop's servant'.

Gilroy: From the Gaelic, meaning 'servant of a red head'.

Giorgio: Italian for 'George'.

Giovanni: Italian for 'John'.

Girald: Mentioned in the Domesday book (11th century), and possibly a variant of 'Gerald'.

Giraldo: Italian for 'Gerald'.

Giraud: French for 'Gerald'.

Giulio: Italian for 'Julius'.

Glanville: From the French, meaning 'one who lives by the oaks'.

Glenn: From the Welsh, meaning a 'green dweller'.

Glynn: From the Welsh, meaning a 'glen dweller'. A variant is *Glyn*.

Godard: French for 'Goddard'.

Goddard: From the German, meaning 'strong in God'.

Godefroi: French for 'Godfrey'.

Goderic: From the German, meaning 'strong in God'.

Godfrey: From the Teutonic, meaning 'peace of God', Mentioned in the Domesday book (11th century).

Godwin: From the Anglo Saxon, meaning a 'friend of God'. A name mentioned in the Domesday book (11th century). Example: *Earl Godwin.*

Goffredo: Italian for 'Godfrey'.

Golding: From the Anglo Saxon, meaning 'son of the golden'.

Gordon: From this Scottish surname, clan name, and place name.

Gorman: From the Celtic, meaning 'of the blue eyes'.

Gottfrid: Swedish for 'Godfrey'.

Gottfried: Dutch and German for 'Godfrey'.

Gotthard: Dutch for 'Goddard'.

Gotthart: German for 'Goddard'.

Gower: From the Gaelic, meaning 'pure'.

Graeme, Graham, Grahame: From the Celtic, and this surname, meaning 'one who lives by the grey land'.

Grainger: From the Anglo Saxon, meaning a 'farmer'.

Grant: From the Anglo Saxon, meaning 'great'.

Granville: From the French, meaning 'of the great town'.

Gregoire: French for 'Gregory'.

Gregoor: Dutch for 'Gregory'.

Gregor: German for 'Gregory'.

Gregorio: Spanish and Italian for 'Gregory'.

Gregory: From the Greek, meaning 'watchful', a variant is Greg.

Greville: From this surname, mentioned in the Battle Abbey Rolls (11th century).

Grey: From the Anglo Saxon, meaning 'grey haired'.

Griffith: From the Celtic, meaning 'red chief'.

Grover: From this surname, and meaning 'one who lived in the grove'.

Gruffydd: Welsh for 'Griffith'.

Guglielmo: Italian for 'William'.

Guido: Swedish, German, Italian and Spanish for 'Guy'. Example: *Guido Fawkes*.

Guilbert: French for 'Gilbert'.

Guillaume: French for 'William'.

Guillermo: Spanish for 'William'.

Guiseppe: Italian for 'Joseph'.

Guistino: Italian for 'Justin'.

Gundolf: Meaning a 'wolf in battle'. Mentioned in the Domesday book (11th century).

Gunther and **Gunter:** From the Norse, meaning 'battle warrior'.

Gustaff: Dutch for 'Gustave'.

Gustav: German for 'Gustave'.

Gustave: From the Swedish, meaning 'Goth's staff'. Variants are *Gus* and *Gustavus*.

Guy: From the German, meaning 'wood'.

Gwilym: Welsh for 'William'.

Gwyn: From the Celtic, meaning 'blond'.

Hadley: From this surname, and meaning 'one who lives by the heath meadow'.

Hadrian: From the Latin, and meaning 'one who is dark'.

Hakon: From the Norse, and meaning 'one of the exalted race'.

Hal: An ancient variant of 'Henry'. King Henry VIII was called 'Bluff King Hal'.

Haldane: From the German, and meaning 'one who is a half Dane'.

Hale: From the Anglo Saxon, and meaning a 'hero'.

Hall: From this surname, and meaning a 'dweller at the hall'. Example: *Hall Caine*.

Halliwell: From the Anglo Saxon, and meaning 'one who dwells by the holy well'.

Hamar: From the Norse, and meaning a 'strong man'.

Hamelin: A name mentioned in the Domesday book (11th century), and meaning a 'home lover'.

Hamilton: From this surname, and meaning 'of the place by the hill'.

Hamish: The Gaelic form of 'James'.

Hamlet: From the Teutonic, meaning the 'son of Hamon'.

Hammond: From this surname, and from the Teutonic, meaning 'belonging to Hamon'.

Hamo: An old Christian name from 'Hammond'. Mentioned in the Hundred Rolls (13th century).

Hamon: An old Anglo Saxon name from 'Heahmund', meaning 'great protection'.

Hank: A variant of 'Henry'. Mainly used in the U.S.A.

Hannibal: From the Phoenician, meaning 'by Baal's grace'. Hannibal was a general of Carthage.

Hans: From the Teutonic 'Johannes' ('John'). Example: *Hans Andersen*.

Harald: Danish and Swedish for 'Harold'.

Harben: From the Gaelic, meaning 'warrior'.

Harcourt: From the French, meaning 'of the fort farm'. This name is mentioned in the Battle Abbey Rolls (11th century).

Harding: From the Teutonic, meaning 'bold friend'.

Hardy: From the Teutonic, meaning 'bold'.

Harold: From the Norse, meaning 'ruler of the army'. Example: *King Harold*.

Harris: From this surname, meaning 'Harry's son'.

Harrison: From this surname, and meaning 'Harry's son'. Example: *Harrison Ford*.

Harry: A variant of 'Henry'.

Hart: From the Anglo Saxon, and meaning 'like a deer'.

Hartford: From the Anglo Saxon, and meaning 'one who lives by the hart's ford'.

Hartley: From this surname, and meaning 'one who lives by the hart's meadow'.

Harvey: From the Teutonic, and meaning a 'warrior'.

Hastings: From the Anglo Saxon, and meaning 'son of a violent man'.

Havelock: From the Norse and meaning a 'sea contestant'.

Hayden: From this surname, and meaning 'one who lived by a hedged wall'.

Heathcliff: From the Anglo Saxon, and meaning 'one who lives by the cliff heath'.

Hector: From the Greek, and meaning 'hold fast'.

Heinrich: German for 'Henry'.

Hendrik: Danish and Dutch for 'Henry'.

Henri: French for 'Henry'.

Henrik: Swedish for 'Henry'.

Henry: From the Teutonic, meaning 'ruler'. Variants are *Hal, Harry, Hank*. Example: *Henry the Eighth*.

Herbert: From the Teutonic, meaning 'brilliant warrior'. Variants are *Bert, Herbie*. Example: *Herbert G. Wells*.

Herbrand: From the Teutonic, meaning 'army's sword'.

Hercules: From the Greek, meaning 'glory of Hera'.

Hereward: From the Anglo Saxon, meaning 'army keeper'. Example: *Hereward the Wake*.

Herman: From the Teutonic, meaning 'warrior'.

Hermon: From the Hebrew, meaning 'sacred'.

Hernando: Spanish for 'Ferdinand'.

Herold: Dutch for 'Harold'.

Hervey: From the Teutonic, meaning a 'warrior'. Mentioned in the Curia Regis Rolls (12th century).

Hew: A variant of 'Hugh'.

Heywood: From the Anglo Saxon, and meaning 'one who lived by a hedged forest'.

Hezekiah: From the Hebrew, meaning 'strong in Jehovah'.

Hilaire: From the Latin, meaning 'cheerful'. Example: *Hilaire Belloc*.

Hilario: Spanish for 'Hilary'.

Hilarius: Danish, Dutch, German and Swedish for 'Hilary'.

Hilary: From the Latin, meaning 'cheerful'.

Hildebrand: From the Teutonic, meaning 'war sword'.

Hillier: From the Teutonic, meaning 'brave in battle'.

Hiram: From the Hebrew, meaning 'most noble'.

Hob: A variant of 'Robert'.

Hobart: From the Teutonic, meaning 'brilliant leader'.

Hogan: From the Irish, meaning 'youthful'.

Hollis: From this surname, and meaning 'one who lived near the holly trees'.

Holman: Meaning 'one who lives by a holm'. (Scandinavian for a 'river island'.) Example: *Holman Hunt.*

Homer: From the Greek, meaning 'security'. Homer was the name of a Greek poet of the 9th century. Mainly used as a Christian name in the U.S.A.

Horace: From the Latin, meaning 'keeper of the hours'. A variant is *Horie.*

Horacio: Spanish for 'Horace'.

Horatio: From the Latin, meaning 'keeper of the hours'. Example: *Horatio, Lord Nelson.*

Horatius: German for 'Horace'.

Horats: Dutch for 'Horace'.

Howard: From the Teutonic, meaning 'strong minded'.

Howe: From the Teutonic, meaning 'high one'.

Howell: From the Welsh, meaning 'one who is alert'.

Hubbard: A variant of 'Hubert'.

Hubert: From the Teutonic, meaning 'bright mind'.

Hugh: From the Teutonic, meaning ' of great thought'. A variant is *Hughie.*

Hugibert: German for 'Hubert'.

Hugo: Dutch, Swedish, Spanish, Danish and German for 'Hugh'.

Hugues: French for 'Hugh'.

Hulbert: From the Teutonic, meaning 'brilliant'.

Humbert: From the Teutonic, meaning a 'bright giant'.

Humfrid: Swedish for 'Humphrey'.

Humfried: Dutch and German for 'Humphrey'.

Humphrey: From the Teutonic, meaning 'peaceful giant'.

Hunfredo: Spanish for 'Humphrey'.

Huxley: From the Anglo Saxon, meaning 'of Hugh's lea'.

Hyde: From the Anglo Saxon, meaning 'from the hide' (a land measure).

Hyman: From the Hebrew, meaning 'man of life'. A variant is Hymie.

Iacovo: Italian for 'Jacob'.

Iain: As 'Ian'.

Ian: Scottish for 'John'.

Idris: From the Welsh, meaning a 'fiery Lord'.

Ignace: French for 'Ignatius'.

Ignacio: Spanish for 'Ignatius'.

Ignatius: From the Latin, meaning 'a fiery one'. Example: *Ignatius Loyola*.

Ignaz: German for 'Ignatius'.

Ignazio: Italian for 'Ignatius'.

Ike: A variant of 'Isaac'.

Ilario: Italian for 'Hilary'.

Ing: From the Scandinavian, meaning 'of the meadow'. A variant is *Ingram*.

Ingram: From the Scandinavian, meaning 'of the meadow'. A variant is *Ing*.

Innis: From the Gaelic, and meaning 'of the river island'.

Ira: From the Hebrew, meaning 'watchful'.

Irvine: As 'Irving'.

Irving: From the Anglo Saxon, meaning 'friend of the sea'.

Isaac: From the Hebrew, meaning 'laughing one'. Variants are *Ike* and *Ikey*. Example: *Sir Isaac Newton*.

Isaacco: Italian for 'Isaac'.

Isidore: From the Greek, meaning the 'gift of Isis'. Example: *Isidore Godfrey*.

Isidoro: Italian for 'Isidore'.

Isidro: Spanish for 'Isidore'.

Ivan: From the Russian for 'John'. Example: *Ivan the Terrible*.

Ives: From Brittany, meaning 'son of the yew bowman'.

Ivo: From the Welsh, meaning 'Lord'.

Izaak: Dutch for 'Isaac'. Example: *Izaak Walton*.

Izzy: A variant of 'Isaac' and Israel'.

Jabez: From the Hebrew, meaning the 'cause of pain'.(1 Chronicles 4.9)

Jack: A variant of 'John'.

Jackson: From this surname, meaning the 'son of Jack'.

Jacob: From the Hebrew, meaning 'one who supplants' (Genesis 25.26). A variant is *Jake*. Example: *Jacob Epstein*.

Jacobo: Spanish for 'Jacob'.

Jacques: French for 'Jacob'.

Jaime: Spanish for 'James'.

Jake: A variant of 'Jacob'.

Jakob: German for 'Jacob'.

James: From the Spanish, meaning 'one who supplants'. Variants are *Jim* and *Jimmy*.

Jan: Dutch for 'John'.

Jarrold: From the old English, meaning 'of the weald'.

Jarvie: Means 'spearman'.

Jarvis: From the Teutonic, meaning 'spearman'.

Jason: From the Greek, meaning 'one who heals'. Jason was a hero in Greek mythology.

Jasper: From the Persian, meaning the 'treasurer'.

Jay: From this surname, and meaning 'bird-like'.

Jean: French for 'John'.

Jed: From the Hebrew, meaning 'one who the Lord loves'.

Jefferson: From the Old English, meaning 'the son of Jeffrey'.

Jeffrey: From the French, meaning 'Peace of God'. A variant is *Jeff*.

Jehoshaphat: Meaning 'Jehovah judges'. A variant is *Josh*.

Jenkin: A Welsh variant of 'John'.

Jéréme: French for 'Jeremy'.

Jeremiah: From the Hebrew, meaning 'Jehovah's appointed'. A variant is *Jerry*.

Jeremias: Spanish for 'Jeremy'.

Jeremy: From the Hebrew, meaning 'Jehovah's appointed'. A variant is *Jerry*.

Jerome: From the Latin, meaning a 'holy name'.

Jervis: As 'Jarvis'.

Jesse: From the Hebrew, meaning 'Jehovah is God'. Jesse was the father of David (Ruth 4.1.2). A variant is *Jess*.

Jethro: From the Hebrew, meaning 'abundance'.

Joab: From the Hebrew, meaning 'Jehovah is Father'.

Job: From the Hebrew, meaning 'one who is persecuted'.

Jocelyn: From the Celtic, meaning 'A Champion'.

Joel: From the Hebrew, meaning 'Jehovah is God'.

Johan: Swedish for 'John'.

Johann: German for 'John'. Example: *Johann S. Bach*.

Johannes: German for 'John'. Example: *Johannes Brahms*.

John: From the Hebrew, meaning 'Jehovah is gracious'. Variants are *Jack* and *Johnny*.

Jolyon: A variant of 'Julian'. Jolyon was the name of a character in John Galsworthy's 'Forsyte Saga'.

Jon: A variant of 'John'.

Jonah: From the Hebrew, meaning a 'dove'.

Jonas: From the Hebrew, meaning a 'dove'.

Jonathan: From the Hebrew, meaning 'Jehovah's gift'. A variant is Jon. Jonathan was the son of Saul. Example: *Jonathan Swift*.

Jordan: From the Hebrew, meaning 'going down'.

Jorge: Spanish for 'George'.

José: Spanish for 'Joseph'.

Joseph: From the Hebrew, meaning 'he shall add'. Variants are *Joe* and *Joey*. Joseph was the son of Jacob (Genesis 30.24).

Josh: A diminutive of 'Joshua'.

Joshua: From the Hebrew, meaning 'Jehovah saves'.

Josiah: From the Hebrew, meaning 'Jehovah supports'. A variant is *Josh*.

Juan: Spanish for 'John'.

Judah: From the Hebrew, meaning 'praised'.

Judas: The Greek form of 'Judah'. Example: *Judas Iscariot*.

Judd and **Jud:** From the Hebrew, meaning 'praised'.

Jude: From the Hebrew, meaning 'praised'.

Jules: French for 'Julius'.

Julian: From the Latin, meaning 'hairy'.

Julio: Spanish for 'Julius'.

Julius: From the Latin, meaning 'bearded'. Example: *Julius Caesar*.

Justin: From the Latin, meaning 'justice'.

Justinian: As 'Justin'.

Karel: Dutch for 'Charles'.

Karl: German for 'Charles'.

Kaspar: From the Persian, meaning 'master of the treasure'.

Kavan: From the Gaelic, meaning 'handsome'.

Kay: From the Scottish, meaning a 'giant'.

Keane: From the Irish, meaning 'long or tall'.

Keefe: From the Gaelic, meaning 'noble'.

Keith: From the Gaelic, meaning a 'man of the battlefield'.

Kelly: From the Irish, meaning 'brave warrior'.

Kelvin: From the Gaelic, meaning 'one who lives by a narrow stream'.

Kendall: From this surname, and meaning 'one who lives by a valley'.

Kendrick: From the Gaelic, meaning 'Henry's son'.

Kenelm: From the Anglo Saxon, meaning 'of the royal helmet'.

Kennard: From the German, meaning 'strong'.

Kennedy: From the Gaelic, meaning 'helmet wearer'.

Kenneth: From the Celtic, meaning 'handsome'.

Kenrick: From the Gaelic, meaning the 'son of Henry'.

Kent: From the Celtic, meaning 'bright'.

Kenyon: From the Gaelic, meaning 'white haired'.

Kern: From the Gaelic, meaning 'dark'.

Kerr: From the Gaelic, meaning 'spear'.

Kevin: From the Irish, meaning 'gentle'.

Kim: From the Anglo Saxon, meaning 'one who rules'.

King: From the Anglo Saxon, meaning a 'ruler'.

Kingsley: From this surname, and meaning 'one who lives by the king's meadow'.

Kirk: From the Old Norse, meaning 'dweller by the church'.

Kirsty: A Scottish name for 'Christopher'.

Kit: A variant of 'Christopher'.

Klemens: German for 'Clement'.

Koenraad: Dutch for 'Conrad'.

Konrad: Swedish for 'Conrad'.

Krispijn: Dutch for 'Crispin'.

Kristian: Swedish for 'Christian'.

Kristofor: Swedish for 'Christopher'.

Kurt: German for 'Conrad'.

Lachlan: From the Gaelic, meaning 'one who is warlike'. A variant is *Lachie*.

Lambert: From the Teutonic, meaning 'of the bright land'. This is mentioned in the Domesday book (11th century). Example: *Lambert Simnel*.

Lamberto: Italian for 'Lambert'.

Lance: A diminutive of 'Lancelot'. From the Teutonic, meaning 'land'.

Lancelot: From the Teutonic, meaning 'land'. Example: *Lancelot Gobbo*.

Larry: A variant of 'Lawrence'.

Lars: A diminutive of 'Larson'.

Larson: From the Scandinavian, meaning the 'son of Lars'.

Laurence: From the Latin, meaning 'of the laurels'. Variants are *Larry* and *Laurie*.

Laurens: Dutch for 'Lawrence'.

Laurent: French for 'Lawrence'.

Lauritz: Danish for 'Lawrence'.

Lawrence : From the Latin, meaning 'of the laurels'. Example: *Lawrence of Arabia*.

Lawry: A variant of 'Lawrence'.

Lawson: From the Anglo Saxon, meaning the 'son of Lawrence'.

Lazarus: From the Hebrew, meaning 'with God's help' (Luke 16.20).

Leander: From the Greek, meaning 'lion man'.

Leandre: French for 'Leander'.

Leandro: Italian for 'Leander'.

Lee: From the Anglo Saxon, meaning 'one who lives by the meadow'.

Leif: From the Norse, meaning 'beloved'.

Leigh: From the Anglo Saxon, meaning 'one who lives by the meadow'. Example: *Leigh Hunt*.

Lemar: Mentioned in the Domesday book (11th century). Means 'famous'.

Lemuel: From the Hebrew, meaning 'devoted to the Lord'.

Lennox: From the Gaelic, meaning 'one who lives by the elm trees'.

Leo: From the Latin, meaning a 'lion'. Example: *Leo Abse*.

Leon: From the French, meaning 'like a lion'. A variant is *Leo*.

Leonard: From the Teutonic, meaning 'strong as a lion'. Variants are *Len* and *Lenny*.

Leonardo: Italian for 'Leonard'. Example: *Leonardo Da Vinci*.

Leonhard: German for 'Leonard'.

Leopold: From the Teutonic, meaning 'people's leader'. A variant is *Leo*.

Leopoldo: Spanish and Italian for 'Leopold'.

Leroy: From the French, meaning 'king'.

Leslie: From the Gaelic, meaning 'one who dwells by a garden pool'. A variant is *Les*.

Lester: From this surname, and meaning a 'man from Leicester'.

Leupold: German for 'Leopold'.

Levi: From the Hebrew, meaning 'joined'. Levi was the son of Jacob.

Levret: From the old French, meaning 'as fast as a hare'. A name mentioned in the Domesday book (11th century).

Levric: A variant of 'Levret'.

Lew: A diminutive of 'Lewis', meaning a 'noted warrior'.

Lewin: The name of an earl mentioned in the Domesday book (11th century). A variant of 'Lewis', and the Welsh 'Llewellyn'.

Lewis: Meaning a 'noted warrior'. Example: *Lewis Carroll.*

Liam: Irish for 'William'.

Lincoln: From this surname, meaning 'one who came from Lincoln.'

Lindley: From this surname, meaning 'one who dwells by the linden meadow'.

Lindsey: From this place in Lincolnshire.

Lionel: From the French, meaning a 'young lion'. A variant is *Leo.*

Lionello: Italian for 'Lionel'.

Lisle: From 'Lisle' in Normandy. This name is mentioned in the Battle Abbey Rolls of the 11th century.

Lister: From this old English surname, meaning a 'dyer'.

Llewellyn: From the Welsh, meaning a 'ruler'. Example: *Llewellyn Davies.*

Lloyd: From the Welsh, meaning 'grey haired'. Example: *D. Lloyd George.*

Lodewijk: Dutch for 'Louis'.

Lon and Lonnie: Variants of 'Lawrence'.

Lorenz: German for 'Lawrence'.

Lorenzo: Spanish and Italian for 'Lawrence'.

Lorn and Lorne: From the Gaelic, meaning a 'warrior'.

Lotario: Italian for 'Luther'.

Lothaire: French for 'Luther'.

Louis: From the Teutonic, meaning a 'noted warrior'. Variants are *Lou* and *Lew*. Example: *Louis Pasteur*.

Lovell: From the Norman French 'Louvel', meaning a 'small wolf'. 'Lovel' is mentioned in the Domesday book (11th century).

Lowell: As 'Lovell'.

Luc: French for 'Luke'.

Luca: Italian for 'Luke'.

Lucan: A variant of 'Luke'.

Lucas: From the Latin, meaning 'light'.

Lucian: From the Latin, meaning 'light'.

Luciano: Italian for 'Lucian'.

Lucien: French for 'Lucian'.

Lucio: Spanish for 'Luke'.

Lucius: A variant of 'Luke'.

Lucretius: From the Latin, meaning 'light'.

Ludovic: A Scottish form of 'Louis', meaning a 'noted warrior'.

Ludvig: Swedish for 'Louis'.

Ludwig: From the Teutonic, meaning 'noted warrior'. German for 'Louis'. Example: *Ludwig van Beethoven*.

Luigi: Italian for 'Louis'.

Lukas: Swedish for 'Luke'.

Luke: From the Latin, meaning 'light', and also a 'man of Lucania' (Italy).

Lutero: Spanish for 'Luther'.

Luther: From the Teutonic, meaning 'noted warrior'.Example: *Luther Burbank*.

Lyle: From the French, meaning 'of the isle'.

Lynden and **Lyndon:** From this surname, meaning 'one who dwells by the linden trees'.

Lynn: From the Celtic, meaning 'of the pool'.

Madoc: From the Welsh, meaning 'fortunate'.

Magnus: From the Latin, meaning 'great and important'.

Makepeace: Means a 'man of peace'. Example: *W. Makepeace Thackeray*.

Malachi: From the Hebrew, meaning a 'messenger' (Malachi 1.2).

Malcolm: From the Gaelic, meaning a 'man of Columb'.

Manfred: From the Old English, meaning 'peaceful'.

Manuel: Spanish for 'Emmanuel'.

Marc: French for 'Mark'.

Marcel: A French name, meaning 'warlike'.

Marcello: Italian for 'Marcel'.

Marcellus: From the Latin, meaning 'warlike'.

Marcelo: Spanish for 'Marcel'.

Marco: Italian for 'Mark'. Example: *Marco Polo*.

Marcos: Spanish for 'Mark'.

Marcus: From the Latin, meaning 'warlike'. A variant is *Mark*. Example: *Marcus Aurelius*.

Mario: From the Latin, meaning 'warlike'.

Marius: From the Latin, meaning 'warlike'.

Mark: From the Latin, meaning 'warlike'. Examples: *St. Mark, Mark Twain.*

Markus: German and Swedish for 'Mark'.

Marlon: From the French, meaning 'hawk like'.

Marmaduke: From the Celtic, meaning a 'servant of Madoc'. This name is mentioned in the Domesday book (11th century).

Marshall: From the Anglo Saxon, meaning a 'steward or the chief horseman'.

Martijn: Dutch for 'Martin'.

Martin: From the Latin, meaning 'warlike', Variants are *Mart, Martyn* and *Marty.* Example: *St. Martin.*

Martino: Spanish and Italian for 'Martin'.

Marty: A variant of 'Martin'.

Mateo: Spanish for 'Matthew'.

Matheson: From this surname, and meaning 'Matthew's son'.

Mathieu: French for 'Matthew'.

Matt: A diminutive of 'Matthew', meaning 'gift of God'.

Mattaeus: Danish for 'Matthew'.

Matteo: Italian for 'Matthew'.

Matthäus: German for 'Matthew'.

Mattheus: Dutch and Swedish for 'Matthew'.

Matthew: From the Latin, meaning 'gift of God'. A variant is *Matt.* Examples: *Matthew Arnold, St. Matthew.*

Mathias: From the Latin, meaning 'gift of God'.

Maulever: From the Norman family name of 'Maulevrier'.

Maurice: From the Latin, meaning 'dark as a moor'. A variant is *Morrie.* Example: *Maurice Materlink.*

Mauricio: Spanish for 'Maurice'.

Maurits: Dutch for 'Maurice'.

Maurizio: Italian for 'Maurice'.

Max: A diminutive of 'Maximilian', meaning 'greatest', and 'Maxwell', meaning 'great'.

Maximilian: From the Latin, meaning 'greatest'. Variants are *Max, Maxie* and *Maxim*.

Maximiliano: Spanish for 'Maximilian'.

Maximilianus: Dutch for 'Maximilian'.

Maximilien: French for 'Maximilian'.

Maximo: Spanish for 'Maximilian'.

Maxwell: From the Anglo Saxon, meaning 'great'.

Maynard: From the Teutonic, meaning 'strong and mighty'.

Mayne: A variant of 'Maynard'.

Mayo: From the Gaelic, meaning 'one who lives by the yew trees'.

Melville: From this surname, and the Anglo Saxon, meaning 'one who lives by the mill place'.

Melvin: From the Anglo Saxon, meaning a 'friend'.

Menard: French for 'Maynard'.

Meredith: From the Celtic, meaning 'Lord'.

Mervyn: From the Welsh, meaning a 'friend'.

Micah: From the Hebrew, meaning 'who is God-like'.

Micha: A form of 'Micah'.

Michael: From the Hebrew, meaning 'who is God-like'. Variants are *Mike, Mick* and *Micky*.

Michel: French for 'Michael'.

Michele: Italian for 'Michael'.

Miguel: Spanish for 'Michael'.

Mikael: Swedish for 'Michael'.

Miles: From the Greek 'Milo', meaning 'strong'. Also from the Teutonic, meaning 'one beloved'.

Milne: From this surname, and meaning 'one who lives by a mill'.

Milo: From the Greek, meaning 'strong'.

Milton: From this surname, and meaning 'one who dwells by a mill'.

Mischa: Slav for 'Michael', and meaning 'one who is God-like'.

Mitchell: From 'Michael', and meaning 'one who is God-like'.

Montague: From the French, and meaning 'one who dwells by a hill'. A variant is *Monty*.

Montgomery: From the French, meaning 'from the castle hill'. A variant is *Monty*.

Monty: A diminutive of 'Montague', meaning 'one who dwells by a hill'.

Moore: From the French, meaning 'like a Moor'.

Morgan: From the Welsh, meaning a 'dweller by the sea'.

Moritz: German for 'Maurice'.

Morley: From this surname, and meaning 'one who dwells by the moor meadow'.

Morrice: A variant of 'Maurice'.

Morris: A variant of 'Maurice'.

Mortimer: From this surname. A variant is *Mort*.

Morton: From this surname, meaning 'one who lives by the town's moor'.

Moses: From the Hebrew, meaning 'taken from the water'. Variants are *Mose* and *Moe*.

Mungo: From the Celtic, meaning 'beloved'.

Murdoch: From the Celtic, meaning 'warrior of the sea'.

Murray: From the Celtic, meaning 'warrior of the sea'.

Nahum: From the Hebrew, meaning 'comforter'.

Napier: From the surname 'Napier', meaning a 'cloth-worker'.

Nash: From this surname, and meaning 'one who lives by the ash tree'.

Natal: Spanish for 'Nöel'.

Natale: Italian for 'Nöel'.

Nataniel: Spanish for 'Nathaniel'.

Nathan: From the Hebrew, meaning 'God's gift' (2 Samuel 7).

Nathaniel: Meaning 'God's gift'. A variant is Nat. Example: *Nathaniel Hawthorne.*

Neal: From the Gaelic, meaning a 'champion'.

Neil: From the Gaelic, meaning a 'champion'.

Nelson: From this surname, meaning 'Nell's son'.

Neville: From the French place 'Neuville'.

Newton: From this surname, and meaning 'one who lives by the new town'.

Nial and Niall: As 'Neil'.

Nicholas: From the Greek, meaning 'victorious'. Variants are *Nick* and *Nicky*. Example: *St. Nicholas* (Santa Claus).

Nick: A diminutive of 'Nicholas'.

Nicol: The Scottish form of 'Nicholas'.

Nicola: Italian for 'Nicholas'.

Nicolas: Spanish for 'Nicholas'.

Nigel: From the Latin, meaning 'black'.

Nikolaus: German for 'Nicholas'.

Nils: Scandinavian for 'Neal'.

Noach: Dutch for 'Noah'.

Noah: From the Hebrew, meaning 'rest' (Genesis 5.29).

Noak: Swedish for 'Noah'.

Noé: Spanish and French for 'Noah'.

Nöel: From the French, and usually given to those born at Christmas time.

Noll: An old variant of 'Oliver'.

Norman: From the Anglo Saxon, meaning a 'Northman'. A variant is *Norm*.

Obadiah: From the Hebrew, meaning the 'servant of God' (Obadiah Chapter 1). A variant is *Obie*.

Octavius: From the Latin, meaning the 'eighth child'.

Odo: The half brother of William the Conqueror was so named. This name is little used today.

Olaf: From the Norse 'Olafr', meaning 'old relic'. This name is mentioned in the Domesday book (11th century). Olaf has been the name of some of the kings of Norway.

Olav: A variant of 'Olaf'.

Oliver: From the Teutonic, meaning 'kind'. A variant is *Olly*. Examples: *Oliver Cromwell, Oliver Twist*.

Oliverio: Spanish for 'Oliver'.

Olivier: French for 'Oliver'.

Oliviero: Italian for 'Oliver'.

Omar: From the Persian, meaning 'first born'. Example: *Omar Khayyam*.

Onefre: Spanish for 'Humphrey'.

Onefredo: Italian for 'Humphrey'.

Onfroi: French for 'Humphrey'.

Orazio: Italian for 'Horace'.

Orlando: Italian for 'Roland'.

Orville: From the French, meaning 'of the golden place'. Example: *Orville Wright*.

Orwin: As 'Erwin'.

Osbern: From the German, meaning 'divine bear'.

Osbert: From the Anglo Saxon, meaning 'God's brightness'. A variant is *Ossie*.

Osborn: From the German, meaning 'divine bear'. This name is mentioned in the Domesday book (11th century).

Oscar: From the German, meaning 'divine spear'. Example: *Oscar Wilde*.

Osmond: From the Anglo Saxon, meaning 'divine shield'.

Osmund: As 'Osmond'.

Oswald: From the Anglo Saxon, meaning 'God's power'. A variant is *Ossie*.

Osward: The name of a landholder mentioned in the Domesday book (11th century). From old English 'Osweald', meaning 'divine power'.

Owen: From the old Welsh, and means 'a youthful warrior'. It is also a well known Welsh surname.

Pablo: Spanish for 'Paul'. Example: *Pablo Picasso*.

Paddy: A variant of 'Patrick', meaning 'noble'.

Paolo: Italian for 'Patrick'.

Pascall: One born at Eastertime.

Pascoe: One born at Eastertime.

Pat: A diminutive of 'Patrick', meaning 'noble'.

Patrice: French for 'Patrick'.

Patricio: Spanish for 'Patrick'.

Patrick: From the Latin, meaning 'noble'. Variants are *Pat* and *Paddy*.

Patrizio: Italian for 'Patrick'.

Patrizius: German for 'Patrick'.

Paul: From the Latin, meaning 'small' (Acts 13.9). Example: *St. Paul*.

Payne: From this surname, meaning a 'pagan or country-man'.

Pedro: Spanish for 'Peter', meaning a 'rock'.

Pepin: From the Teutonic, meaning 'to endure'. Pepin was the father of Charlemagne.

Percival: From the French, meaning 'one who pierces the vale'. Variants are *Percy* and *Perce*. Examples: *Percy Grainger, Percy Bysshe Shelley*.

Peregrine: From the Latin, meaning 'wanderer'.

Peret: A forester with this name occurs in the Domesday book (11th century).

Perry: From this surname, and meaning 'of the pear tree'.

Peter: From the Latin, meaning a 'rock'. This name is mentioned in the Domesday book (11th century). A variant is *Pete*. Example: *St. Peter*.

Petrus: German for 'Peter'.

Philemon: From the Greek, meaning 'friendly'.

Philip: From the Greek, meaning 'one who loves horses'. An apostle in the Bible (John 1.43). A variant is *Phil*. Examples: *Prince Philip, Sir Philip Sydney, King Philip of Spain*.

Philippe: French for 'Philip'.

Phineas: From the Greek, meaning 'mouth of the serpent'. Example: *Phineas T. Barman*.

Pierce: From the French 'Piers', and meaning a 'rock'.

Pierpoint: From the Norman family name of 'Pierrepont'.

Pierre: French for 'Peter'. Example: *Pierre Curie*.

Piers: Meaning a 'rock'. Example: *Piers Plowman*.

Pieter: Dutch for 'Peter'.

Pietro: Italian for 'Peter'.

Pip: An old variant of 'Philip'.

Plato: From the Greek, meaning 'broad'. Plato was a Greek philosopher of the 4th century.

Presley: Meaning 'one who dwells at the priest's meadow'. From the Anglo Saxon.

Prester: Meaning 'one who is a priest'.

Pugh: From the Welsh, meaning the 'son of Hugh'.

Quentin: From the Latin, meaning the 'fifth child'.

Quiller: From the Gaelic, meaning a 'cub'.

Quincy: From the French, meaning 'connected to the fifth son'.

Quinn: From the Irish, meaning 'wise'.

Quinton: From the Latin, meaning the 'fifth child'.

Rab: A Scottish form of 'Robert'. From the Anglo Saxon, meaning 'famous and brilliant'.

Raban: From the old German, meaning 'raven'.

Radley: From this surname, meaning 'one who lives by the red meadow'.

Rafael: Spanish for 'Raphael'.

Rafaelle: Italian for 'Raphael'.

Raimondo: Italian for 'Raymond'.

Raimund: German for 'Raymond'.

Ralph: From the Anglo Saxon, meaning 'wolf's shield'. A variant is *Rolph*. Example: *Ralph Waldo Emerson*.

Ramon: Spanish for 'Raymond'. Example: *Ramon Navarro*.

Ramsay: From the Scottish, meaning 'from the ram's island'.

Ranald: A Scottish form of 'Ronald', meaning 'mighty and powerful'.

Randall: From the German, meaning 'wolf's shield'.

Randolph: From the German, meaning 'wolf's shield'. A variant is *Randy*.

Ranulf: A variant of 'Ralph'. Mentioned in the Domesday book (11th century): 'Ralph' meaning 'shield of a wolf'.

Raoul: French for 'Ralph', meaning 'wolf's shield'.

Raphael: From the Hebrew, meaning 'healing of God'.

Rastus: A variant of 'Erastus'.

Rawnsley: Meaning 'one who lives by the raven's meadow'.

Ray: A diminutive of 'Raymond', meaning 'great protector'.

Raymond: From the Teutonic, meaning 'great protector'.

Rayne: From the Scandinavian, meaning 'mighty army'.

Rayner: From the Scandinavian, meaning 'mighty army'.

Redmond: From the Anglo Saxon, meaning 'protecting counsel'.

Reece: From the Welsh, meaning 'ardent'.

Reeve: From this surname, meaning a 'bailiff'.

Reginald: From the Anglo Saxon, meaning 'powerful ruler'. Variants are *Reg* and *Reggie*.

Reinald: An 11th century name little used today. Possibly the same as 'Ronald', and the early English surname 'Reynold'.

Reinbert: A name little used today, but this was the name of a landholder recorded in the Domesday book (11th century).

Reinhold: Danish and Swedish for 'Reginald'.

Reinold: Dutch for 'Reginald'.

Reinwald: German for 'Reginald'.

Remus: From the Latin, meaning a 'power'. Romulus and Remus are said to have founded Rome.

Renaldo: Spanish for 'Ronald'.

Renato: Spanish for 'Reginald'.

Renault: French for 'Reginald'.

Rendle: The same as 'Randall'.

René: French for 'Reginald'.

Reuben: From the Hebrew, meaning a 'son is born'. A variant is *Rube*. Reuben was the son of Leah and Jacob.

Rex: From the Latin, meaning a 'king'.

Rey: Spanish for 'Rex'.

Rhys: Welsh, meaning 'ardent'. Example: *Rhys Davies*.

Ricardo: Spanish for 'Richard'.

Riccardo: Italian for 'Richard'.

Richard: From the Teutonic, meaning a 'ruler of power'. This name is mentioned in the Domesday book (11th century). Variants are *Dick, Dickie, Ritchie, Ricky*. Example: *Richard Coeur de Lion*.

Richie: A Scottish form of 'Richard', meaning 'ruler of power'.

Ricky: A variant of 'Richard', meaning 'ruler of power'.

Rider: From the Anglo Saxon, meaning a 'horseman'. Example: *Rider Haggard*.

Rigg: From this surname, meaning 'one who lived by the ridge'.

Rinaldo: Italian for 'Reginald'.

Riordan: From the Irish, meaning a 'bard'.

Ritchie: A variant of 'Richard', meaning 'ruler of power'.

Robert: From the Anglo Saxon, meaning 'famous and brilliant'. Variants are *Bob, Bobby, Robin, Rob, Robby, Rab.* Example: *Robert Burns.*

Roberto: Spanish and Italian for 'Robert'.

Robin: A form of 'Robert', meaning 'famous and brilliant'. A variant is *Rob.* Examples: *Robin Goodfellow* in 'A Midsummer Night's Dream', *Robin Hood.*

Robinson: From this surname, meaning 'son of Robin'. Variants are *Rob, Robin.* Example: *Robinson Crusoe.*

Rod: From 'Roderick', meaning 'great ruler'.

Roderich: German for 'Roderick'.

Roderick: From the German, meaning 'great ruler'. Variants are *Rod, Roddy, Ricky.*

Rodger: From the Teutonic, meaning 'great spearman'.

Rodney: From the Anglo Saxon, meaning 'one from the island of reeds'. A variant is *Rod.* Example: *Rodney Stone.*

Rodolfo: Spanish and Italian for 'Rudolph'.

Rodolphe: French for 'Rudolph'.

Rodrigo: Italian for 'Roderick'.

Rodrigue: French for 'Roderick'.

Roeland: Dutch for 'Roland'.

Rogan: From this surname.

Roger: From the Teutonic, meaning 'great spearman'. A variant is *Rodge.* Examples: *Roger Casement, Sir Roger de Coverley.*

Rogerio: Spanish for 'Roger'.

Roi: French for 'Rex'.

Roland: From the Teutonic, meaning 'famed in the land'. Variants are *Rowland, Rowe,* and *Rolly.*

Rolando: Spanish for 'Roland'.

Rolf and **Rolph:** From the Teutonic, meaning 'famous wolf'.

Rolland: A variant of 'Roland' and a name mentioned in the Domesday book (11th century).

Rollo: From the Latin, meaning 'famous wolf'.

Romeo: From the Italian, meaning a 'man of Rome'. Example: *Romeo and Juliet* in Shakespeare's play.

Ronald: From the Teutonic, meaning 'powerful and mighty'. Variants are *Ron* and *Ronnie*.

Rory: From the Irish, meaning 'red king'.

Roscoe: From the Norse, meaning 'one from the forest of deer'.

Ross: From the Scottish, meaning 'of the peninsula'.

Rowe: A variant of 'Roland', meaning 'famed in the land'.

Rowland: From the Teutonic, meaning 'famed in the land'. A variant is *Rowe*. Example: *Rowland Hill*.

Rowley: From the Anglo Saxon, meaning 'one who dwells by the old meadow'. A variant is *Rowe*.

Roy: From the Celtic, meaning 'red' and from the French for 'king'.

Rubén: Spanish for 'Reuben'.

Rüdiger: German for 'Roger'.

Rudolf: German for 'Rudolph'.

Rudolph: From the Teutonic, meaning 'famous wolf'. Variants are *Rudy* and *Rudi*.

Rudy: A variant of 'Rudolph'.

Rudyard: From the Anglo Saxon, meaning 'from the area of the reeds'. A variant is *Rudd*. Example: *Rudyard Kipling*.

Ruff: A variant of 'Rufus'.

Rufus: From the Latin, meaning 'red haired'. A variant is *Ruff*. Example: *King Rufus of England*.

Ruggiero: Italian for 'Roger'.

Rupert: From the Teutonic, meaning 'famous and bright'. Example: *Rupert Brooke*.

Ruprecht: German for 'Robert'.

Rurik: From the Slav for 'Roderick'.

Russ: A variant of 'Russell'.

Russell: From the French, meaning 'red haired'. A variant is *Russ*.

Rutger: Dutch for 'Roger'.

Ruy: Spanish for 'Roderick'.

Salomo: Dutch and German for 'Solomon'.

Salomon: French for 'Solomon', meaning 'peaceful'.

Salomone: Italian for 'Solomon', meaning 'peaceful'.

Salvador: From the Spanish, meaning the 'Saviour'. Example: *Salvador Dali*.

Salvatore: Italian for 'Salvador'.

Sampson: From the Hebrew, meaning 'as the sun'.

Samson: From the Hebrew, meaning 'as the sun' (Judges 13.16). Variants are *Sam* and *Sammy*.

Samuel: From the Hebrew, meaning 'of God'. Variants are *Sam* and *Sammy*. Examples: *Samuel Pepys, Samuel Johnson*.

Samuele: Italian for 'Samuel'.

Sancho: From the Spanish, meaning 'sanctified'. Example: *Sancho Panza* in 'Don Quixote'.

Sanders: Meaning the 'son of Alexander-defender'. A variant is *Sandy*.

Sansón: Spanish for 'Samson'.

Sansone: Italian for 'Samson'.

Saul: From the Hebrew, meaning 'who is asked for' (1 Samuel 9.2). Example: *Saul of Tarsus*.

Saveur: French for 'Salvador'.

Scott: From this surname, and meaning 'one coming from Scotland'.

Sean: Irish for 'John', meaning 'God is gracious'. Example: *Sean O'Casey*.

Seaton: From this surname, and meaning 'one who lives at a sea town'.

Sebastian: From the Greek, meaning 'venerable'. Example: *Sebastian Cabot*.

Sebastiano: Italian for 'Sebastian'.

Sébastien: French for 'Sebastian'.

Selby: From the Anglo Saxon, meaning 'one who lives by the willows'.

Selwyn: From the Anglo Saxon, meaning 'of the woods'.

Septimus: Meaning the 'seventh son'. Example: *Septimus Burton*.

Seth: From the Hebrew, meaning 'one appointed'.

Seton: A variant of 'Seaton'.

Sewald: A variant of 'Sewell'.

Seward: From the old French, meaning 'guardian of the sea'.

Sewell: From the Anglo Saxon, meaning a 'powerful sea man'.

Seymour: From this surname, and the town 'St. Maur' in France.

Shamus: The Irish for 'James', meaning 'one who supplants'.

Shane: Irish for 'John'.

Shaw: From the Anglo Saxon, meaning 'of the wood'.

Sherlock: Meaning 'of the white or shorn locks'. Example: *Sherlock Holmes*.

Sherman: From the Anglo Saxon, meaning a 'wool man'.

Sholto: From the Gaelic, meaning a 'sower'.

Sidney: From the old English 'Sidony', and from this surname, meaning 'one who lives on a great island'.

Siegfried: From the Teutonic, meaning 'victorious'. Siegfried was a hero in some of the German legends.

Siffre: French for 'Siegfried'.

Sigismond: French for 'Sigmund'.

Sigismondo: Italian for 'Sigmund'.

Sigismund: From the Teutonic, meaning ' protector of victory'.

Sigismundo: Spanish for 'Sigmund'.

Sigismundus: Dutch for 'Sigmund'.

Sigmund: From the Teutonic, meaning 'protector of victory'.

Sigvard: Norwegian for 'Siegfried'.

Silas: From the Latin, meaning 'of the forests'. Example: *Silas Marner*.

Silvain: French for 'Silvanus'.

Silvester: From the Latin, meaning 'of the forests'.

Silvestre: Spanish and French for 'Silvester'.

Silvestro: Italian for 'Silvester'.

Silvio: Spanish and Italian for 'Silvanus'.

Sim: A diminutive of 'Simeon', meaning 'one who hearkens'.

Simeon: From the Hebrew, meaning 'one who hearkens'. French for 'Simon'. Variants are *Sim* and *Simmy*.

Simon: Greek for the Hebrew 'Simeon', meaning 'one who hearkens'. Variants are *Sim* and *Simmy*. Examples: *Simon Bolivar* and *Simon de Montfort*.

Simone: Italian for 'Simon'.

Sinclair: From the surname, and the place 'St. Clair' in France.

Solomon: From the Hebrew, meaning 'peaceful' (2 Samuel 5.14). Variants are *Sol* and *Solly*. Example: *King Solomon*.

Somerset: From this surname, and from the county.

Spencer: From the old English, meaning a 'dispenser of goods'.

St. Barbe: A name mentioned in the Rolls of Battle Abbey (11th century) and from this village in Normandy.

St. John: From 'Saint John' (usually pronounced 'Sinjon').

Stafford: From the Anglo Saxon, meaning 'from the landing place'.

Stanford: From the Anglo Saxon, meaning 'one who lives by the ford's stones'. A variant is *Stan*.

Stanislaus: From the Polish, meaning 'glorious'.

Stanley: From the Anglo Saxon, meaning 'one who dwells in the stone meadow'. A variant is *Stan*.

Stefan: German for 'Stephen'.

Stefano: Italian for 'Stephen'.

Stephanus: Swedish for 'Stephen'.

Stephen: From the Greek, meaning 'crowned' (Acts 6.5). Variants are *Steve* and *Stevie*. Examples: *St. Stephen, Stephen Foster* and *Stephen Langton*.

Steven: As 'Stephen', meaning 'crowned'.

Stewart: From the Anglo Saxon, meaning a 'steward'. A variant is *Stew*.

Stratford: From the Anglo Saxon, meaning 'one who lives by the ford - near the street'.

Sutton: Meaning 'one who comes from a southern town'.

Swithin: Means 'swift and strong'. Example: *St. Swithin*.

Sydney: From the old English 'Sidony', and also from 'one who lives on a great island'. A variant is Syd. Example: *Sydney Carlton*.

Sylvanus: From the Latin, meaning 'of the forests'.

Sylvester: From the Latin, meaning 'of the forests'.

Taddeo: Italian for 'Thaddeus', meaning 'praiseworthy'.

Tadeo: Spanish for 'Thaddeus'.

Taffy: From the Welsh, meaning 'one who is loved'. A form of 'David'.

Talbot: From this surname, meaning 'one who commands the valley'.

Tam and **Tammy:** Scottish forms of 'Tom', meaning a 'twin'. Example: *Tam O'Shanter* by Robert Burns.

Ted and **Teddie:** Variants of 'Theodore' and 'Edward'. Meaning 'one who guards the treasure'.

Tedric: The name of a landowner mentioned in the Domesday book (11th century). Probably today's 'Cedric'.

Teobaldo: Italian and Spanish for 'Theobald'.

Teodoro: Italian and Spanish for 'Theodore'.

Terence: From the Latin, meaning 'one who has polished manners'.

Terencio: Spanish for 'Terence'.

Terriss: A variant of 'Terence'.

Terry: A variant of 'Terence'.

Thaddäus: German for 'Thaddeus'.

Thaddeus: From the Greek, meaning 'praiseworthy'.

Theobald: From the Teutonic, meaning 'of the bold people'.

Theodor: Swedish, Danish and German for 'Theodore'.

Theodore: From the Greek, meaning a 'man whom God gives'. Variants are *Theo*, *Ted*, *Teddy*.

Theodoric: From the Teutonic, meaning 'one who rules the people'.

Theodorus: Dutch for 'Theodore'.

Thewlis: Probably from 'Hugh'. A name mentioned in the records of Somerset House, London (1902).

Thibaut: French for 'Theobald'.

Thomas: From the Hebrew, meaning a 'twin'. Variants are *Tom, Tommy, Tam, Tammy*. Examples: *Thomas Edison, Thomas a' Becket*.

Thorold: From the Norse, meaning 'ruled by Thor'.

Thurstan: From the Norse, meaning 'Thor's stone'.

Tibold: German for 'Theobald'.

Tiebout: Dutch for 'Theobald'.

Tim: A diminutive of 'Timothy', meaning 'honouring God'.

Timon: From the Greek, meaning a 'reward'. Example: Shakespeare's *'Timon of Athens'*.

Timoteo: Italian for 'Timothy'.

Timothée: French for 'Timothy'.

Timotheus: German for 'Timothy'.

Timothy: From the Greek, meaning 'honouring God'. Variants are *Tim* and *Timmy*. Example: *St. Timothy*.

Tite: French for 'Titus'.

Tito: Italian and Spanish for 'Titus'.

Titus: From the Greek, meaning 'honour' (Galatians 2.3). Example: *Titus Oates*.

Tobia: Italian for 'Tobias'.

Tobias: From the Hebrew, meaning 'God is good'.

Tobie: French for 'Tobias'.

Toby: From the Hebrew, meaning 'God is good'.

Tom and **Tommy:** Variants of 'Thomas', meaning a 'twin'.

Tomás: Spanish for 'Thomas'.

Tomaso: Italian for 'Thomas'.

Travers: From this surname, and meaning 'one who lives at the cross roads'.

Trent: From the Celtic, meaning 'one who lives by a stream'.

Trevor: From the Welsh, meaning 'of the homestead'. A variant is Trev.

Tristam: From the Welsh, meaning 'one who makes a noise'. Example: *Tristam Shandy*.

Uberto: Italian for 'Hubert'.

Ugo: Italian for 'Hugh'.

Ulises: Spanish for 'Ulysses'.

Ulmer: From the Norse, meaning 'wolf man'. This was the name of a priest in the Domesday book (11th century).

Ulric: From the Teutonic, meaning 'ruler of the wolves'.

Ulward: From the Norse, meaning 'wolf watcher'.

Ulwin: Means 'wolf's friend'. This name is mentioned in the Domesday book (11th century).

Ulysses: From the Greek, meaning 'one who hates'.

Umberto: Italian for 'Humbert'.

Urbaine: French for 'Urban'.

Urban: From the Latin, meaning 'of the city'.

Urbano: Italian and Spanish for 'Urban'.

Uriah: From the Hebrew, meaning 'light of God' (Samuel 11.1). Example: *Uriah Heep.*

Val: A diminutive of 'Valentine', meaning 'strong'.

Valdemar: From the Teutonic, meaning a 'noted ruler'. A variant is *Val*.

Valentijn: Dutch for 'Valentine'.

Valentin: French, Spanish, German, Danish and Swedish for 'Valentine'.

Valentine: From the Latin, meaning 'strong'. A variant is *Val*. Example: *St. Valentine*.

Valentino: Italian for 'Valentine'.

Van: A Dutch forename, meaning 'from...'. Example: *Van Johnson*.

Vance: From the Anglo Saxon, meaning 'young'.

Vassily: Russian for 'Basil', meaning 'kingly'.

Vaughan: From the Welsh, meaning 'small'. Example: *Vaughan Williams*.

Vere: From the place 'Ver' in Caen. This name is mentioned in the Domesday book (11th century).

Vernon: From the Latin, meaning 'young'.

Vesey: From the Norman family 'de Vesci'.

Vicente: Spanish for 'Vincent'.

Victor: From the Latin, meaning a 'conqueror'. A variant is *Vic*. Example: *Victor Hugo*.

Vilhelm: Swedish for 'William'.

Vince: From the Latin, meaning 'conqueror'. Example: *Vince Hill*.

Vincent: From the Latin, meaning a 'conqueror'. A variant is *Vince*.

Vincente: Italian for 'Vincent'.

Vincentius: Dutch for 'Vincent'.

Vincenz: German for 'Vincent'

Viney: A variant of 'Vincent'.

Vinny: A variant of 'Vincent'.

Virgil: From the Latin, meaning 'staff bearer'.

Virgilio: Italian and Spanish for 'Virgil'.

Vitorio: Spanish for 'Victor'.

Vittorio: Italian for 'Victor'.

Vivian: From the Latin, meaning 'lively'. A variant is *Viv*.

Waldo: From the Teutonic, meaning 'ruler'. Example: *Ralph Waldo Emerson*.

Walford: From the Anglo Saxon, meaning 'of the Welsh ford'.

Wallace: Meaning a 'man who comes from Wales'. A variant is

Wally.

Wallache: German for 'Wallace'.

Wallis: Meaning a 'man who comes from Wales'.

Walt: A variant of 'Walter'. Example: *Walt Whitman.*

Walter: From the Teutonic, meaning 'ruler of the army'. This name is mentioned in the Domesday book (11th century). Variants are *Wat* and *Walt*. Example: *Sir Walter Scott.*

Walther: German for 'Walter'.

Ward: From the Anglo Saxon, meaning a 'guardian'.

Warne: A variant of 'Warner', meaning a 'warrior'.

Warner: From the Teutonic, meaning a 'warrior'.

Warren: From the Teutonic, meaning a 'watchman'. This name is mentioned in the Rolls of Battle Abbey (11th century).

Washington: From this Anglo Saxon place name. Example: *Washington Irving.*

Wat: A variant of 'Walter'. Example: *Wat Tyler.*

Wayne: From the Anglo Saxon, meaning a 'waggoner'.

Webster: From the Anglo Saxon, meaning a 'weaver'.

Wenceslaus: From the Slav, meaning 'crowned with glory'. Example: *Good King Wenceslaus.*

Wendell: From the Teutonic, meaning a 'wanderer'.

Werner: German for 'Warner'.

Wesley: From the Anglo Saxon, meaning 'one who lives at the west meadow'.

Whitney: From the Anglo Saxon, meaning 'one who lives at the white island'.

Whittaker: From the Anglo Saxon, meaning 'one who lives at the white acre'.

Wibert: A rare Christian name today but one which was the name of a landholder mentioned in the Domesday book (11th century).

Wilbur: From the Teutonic, meaning 'one who is brilliant'. A name used a lot in America.

Wilfred: From the Teutonic, meaning a 'man of peace'. A variant is *Wilf*.

Wilhelm: German for 'William'.

Willem: Dutch for 'William'.

Willemot: From the old German, meaning 'resolute of spirit'. This name is mentioned in the records in Devon in the 12th century.

William: From the Teutonic, meaning 'strong protector'. Variants are *Bill, Billie, Will, Willie*. This was a very popular name at the time of William the Conqueror. Examples: *William Shakespeare, William the Conqueror, William Wordsworth*.

Wilmer: From the Teutonic, meaning 'famous'.

Wilson: From this surname, meaning 'Will's son'.

Winston; From the Anglo Saxon, meaning 'from the estate of a friend'.

Wolf and **Wolfe:** From the Anglo Saxon, meaning a 'wolf'.

Wolfgang: From the Teutonic, meaning 'bold wolf'. Example: *Wolfgang Goethe*.

Woodrow: From the Anglo Saxon, meaning 'one who lives by the hedge row'.

Wulfric: From the Anglo Saxon, meaning 'wolf's ruler'.

Wulfstone: From the Anglo Saxon, meaning 'wolf's stone'.

Wynn and **Wynne:** From the Celtic, meaning 'white'.

Xavier: From the Spanish, meaning 'new house owner'.

Xenophon: From the Greek, meaning 'one who kills strangers'.

Xerxes: From the Persian, meaning 'royal ruler'. Example: *Xerxes was the King of Persia* in the 5th century B.C.

Yale: From the Anglo Saxon, meaning 'from the corner slope'.

Yehudi: From the Hebrew, meaning 'the Lord praises'.

Yule: Originally given to a boy born at Christmas.

Yves: From the old Breton, meaning 'well born'.

Zacarias: Spanish for 'Zachary'.

Zaccaria: Italian for 'Zachary'.

Zachariah: From the Hebrew, meaning 'Jehovah has remembered'. Variants are *Zack* and *Zachary*.

Zacharias: German for 'Zachary'.

Zacharie: French for 'Zachary'.

Zachary: From the Hebrew, meaning 'Jehovah has remembered'. A variant is *Zack*.

Zakarias: Swedish for 'Zachary'.

Zane: A variant of 'John', meaning 'God is gracious'.

Zebadiah: From the Hebrew, meaning 'Jehovah has given' (1 Chronicles 8.15). A variant is *Zebby*.

Zebedee: From the Greek, meaning 'my gift'.

Zebulon: From the Hebrew, meaning 'dwelling place'.

Zekiel: A diminutive of 'Ezekiel', meaning 'God's strength'.

GIRLS' NAMES

Abbie: A variant of 'Abigail', meaning 'of the father of joy', from the Hebrew 'Abigayil'.

Abigail: From the Hebrew, meaning 'of the father of joy'. Little used today. Variants are *Abbey*, *Abby* and *Gail*.

Acacia: From the Greek 'Akakia', and the plant of this name.

Ada: From the early English 'Acada', meaning 'happy one'.

Adah: From the Hebrew, meaning an 'ornament'. Mentioned in Genesis 4.19.

Adalia: From the old German 'Adal', meaning 'noble'.

Addie: A variant of 'Adelaide', meaning 'noble'.

Addy: A variant of 'Adelaide', meaning 'noble'.

Adel: Mentioned in the Somerset House records of 1905. From the Teutonic, meaning 'noble'.

Adela: From the Germanic, meaning 'noble'. This was the name of a daughter of William the Conqueror.

Adelaide: From the Germanic, meaning 'noble'. Variants are *Addie* and *Della*.

Adèle: French for 'Adela', meaning 'noble'.

Adelheid: German for 'Adelaide', meaning 'noble'.

Adelicia: A variant of 'Adelaide', meaning 'noble'.

Adelina: French, Spanish and Italian for 'Adela', meaning 'noble'.

Adeline: A variant of 'Adela', meaning 'noble'.

Adelle: From the old German, meaning 'noble'.

Adora: From the Latin 'Adoria', meaning 'one adored'.

Adriana: A feminine form of 'Adrian', meaning 'one who came from the Adriatic'.

Adriane: A German feminine form of 'Adrian', meaning 'one who came from the Adriatic'.

Adrienne: A feminine form of 'Adrian', meaning 'one who came from the Adriatic'.

Agata: Italian for 'Agatha'. From the Greek, meaning 'good'.

Agatha: From the Greek, and meaning 'good'. St. Agatha was martyred in Sicily in the 3rd century. A variant is *Aggie*.

Agathe: French for 'Agatha', meaning 'good'.

Agave: From the Greek, meaning 'noble'. Agave was the daughter of Cadmus in a Greek legend.

Aggie: A variant of 'Agatha', meaning 'good'.

Agnes: From the Greek 'Agnos', meaning 'pure'. St. Agnes was martyred at the time of Diocletian. Variants are *Aggie*, *Nessa*, *Nessie*.

Agneta: Danish and Swedish for 'Agnes', meaning 'pure'.

Agueda: Spanish for 'Agatha', meaning 'good'.

Aida: A variant of 'Ada'.

Aileen: Irish for 'Helen' and 'Ellen', meaning 'bringing light'.

Aimée: French for 'Amy', meaning 'beloved'.

Alaine: A variant of 'Alanna', meaning 'beautiful'.

Alanna: Gaelic, and meaning 'beautiful'. Variants are *Lana* and *Alaine*.

Alarice: From the old German, meaning 'ruler'.

Alberta: The feminine form of 'Albert', meaning 'bright and noble'.

Albertina: A variant of 'Alberta', and meaning 'bright and noble'.

Albinia: From the Latin, and meaning 'blond'. Variants are *Alvina and Albina.*

Alcina: From the Greek 'Alkino', meaning 'strong willed'.

Alda: From the Anglo Saxon, meaning 'old'.

Aldyth: From the Anglo Saxon 'Aeldgyth', meaning 'old'.

Alejandra: Spanish for 'Alexandra', meaning 'man's helper'.

Alena: A variant of 'Adela', meaning 'noble'.

Alene: A variant of 'Aileen', meaning 'bringing light'.

Alessandra: Italian for 'Alexandra', meaning 'man's helper'.

Aleta: Spanish for 'Alida', meaning 'birdlike'.

Aletta: Italian for 'Alida', meaning 'birdlike'.

Alex: A variant of 'Alexandra', meaning 'man's helper'.

Alexandra: A feminine form of 'Alexander'. From the Greek, meaning 'man's helper'. Example: *Queen Alexandra*, wife of Edward VII.

Alexandrina: A variant of 'Alexandra', meaning 'man's helper'.

Alexandrine: French for 'Alexandra', meaning 'man's helper'.

Alexina: From the masculine 'Alex'. Sometimes used in Scotland.

Alexine: A variant of 'Alexandra', meaning 'man's helper'.

Alexis: A variant of 'Alexandra', meaning 'man's helper'.

Alfa: A variant of 'Alpha', a name from the Greek, and given to the first born.

Alfonsine: From the old German 'Adal-funs', meaning 'noble and ready'.

Alfreda: A feminine form of 'Alfred', and meaning 'elves' counsel'. A variant is *Freda*.

Alice: From the Teutonic, and meaning 'noble'. Variants are *Allie* and *Alicia*.

Alicia: A variant of 'Alice', meaning 'noble'.

Alida: Means 'birdlike'.

Alie: A variant of 'Alison', meaning 'noble'.

Alima: From the Arabic, meaning 'a lover of music and dancing'.

Alina: A variant of 'Alanna', and meaning 'beautiful'.

Aline: A variant of 'Adela', meaning 'noble'.

Alison: A variant of 'Alice', and meaning 'noble'.

Alita: A variant of 'Alida', meaning 'bird like'.

Allie: A variant of 'Alice', meaning 'noble'.

Allys: A variant of 'Alice', meaning 'noble'.

Alma: Meaning 'of the soul'.

Almira: A name which comes from the Middle East, and means 'truthful'.

Alonza: A feminine form of 'Alonzo', meaning 'noble'.

Alpha: From the Greek, and usually given to the first born child.

Althea: From the Greek, meaning 'a flower'.

Alvera: A name very little used today but the name of a free woman mentioned in the Domesday book (11th century).

Alvina: A variant of 'Albina', meaning 'blond'.

Amabel: A variant of 'Mabel', meaning 'beloved'. Variants are *Amabella* and *Mab*.

Amalea: A variant of 'Amelia', meaning 'industrious'.

Amalia: Dutch, German and Spanish for 'Amelia', meaning 'industrious'.

Amanda: From the Latin, and meaning 'to be loved'.

Amaryllis: From the Greek, and meaning 'rippling stream'.

Amata: Spanish, Swedish and Italian for 'Amy', meaning 'beloved'.

Amelia: From the Teutonic 'Amalie', and meaning 'industrious'. Variants are *Amy, Emmy* and *Emmie*.

Amelie: French for 'Amelia', meaning 'industrious'.

Amethyst: From the Greek, meaning 'of wine colour'.

Amy: Meaning 'beloved'.

Anastasia: From the Greek, meaning 'risen again'.

Anastasie: French for 'Anastasia', meaning 'risen again'.

Andrea: A feminine form of 'Andrew', meaning 'manly and strong'.

Andria: A girl from the Greek island of Andros.

Andriana: A variant of 'Andrew', meaning 'manly and strong'.

Angela: From the Greek, meaning an 'angel'. A variant is *Angie*.

Angele: French for 'Angela', meaning an 'angel'.

Angelica: From the Latin, meaning 'angelic'.

Angelika: Greek for 'Angelica', and meaning 'angelic'.

Angelina: A variant of 'Angela', meaning an 'angel'.

Angeline: A variant of 'Angela', meaning an 'angel'.

Angelique: French for 'Angelica', meaning 'angelic'.

Angie: A diminutive of 'Angela', meaning an 'angel'.

Anita: A variant of 'Anne', and meaning 'graceful'.

Anna: Dutch, Italian, German, Swedish and Danish for 'Anne', meaning 'graceful'.

Annabel: A variant of 'Anna', meaning 'graceful'.

Annabella: A variant of 'Anna', meaning 'graceful'.

Anne: From the Hebrew 'Hannah', meaning 'graceful'. Variants are *Ann, Annie* and *Nan.* Example: *Anne Boleyn.*

Annette: A variant of 'Anne', meaning 'graceful'.

Annuciata: From the Latin, meaning 'news bearer'.

Annunziata: Italian for 'Annunciata', meaning 'news bearer'.

Anona: From the Latin, meaning 'fruitful'.

Anstice: A variant of 'Anastasia', meaning 'risen again'.

Anthea: From the Greek 'Anthos', meaning a 'flower'.

Antoinette: French for 'Antonia', meaning 'without price'.

Antonia: From the Latin, meaning 'without price'.

Antonie: German for 'Antonia', meaning 'without price'.

Antonietta: Italian for 'Antonia', meaning 'without price'.

Anunciacion: Spanish for 'Annunciata', meaning 'news bearer'.

April: From the month, and usually given to one born in this month.

Arabela: Spanish for 'Arabella', and meaning 'prayerful'.

Arabella: From the Latin, meaning 'prayerful'.

Arabelle: German for 'Arabella', and meaning 'prayerful'.

Araminta: A variant of 'Arabella', and 'Aminta', meaning 'prayer and protection'.

Ardelle: From the Latin, meaning 'enthusiastic'.

Ardene: A variant of 'Ardelle', meaning 'enthusiastic'.

Areta: From the Greek, meaning 'virtuous'.

Arette: French for 'Areta', meaning 'virtuous'.

Ariadne: From the Latin 'Ariadna', meaning 'to please'.

Ariana: From the Latin 'Ariadna', meaning 'to please'.

Arleen: From the Gaelic, meaning a 'promise'.

Arlene: From the Gaelic, meaning a 'promise'.

Arlette: A variant of 'Arlene', meaning a 'promise'.

Astra: From the Greek, meaning a 'star'.

Astrid: From the old Norse, meaning 'Godly strength'.

Atalanta: From the Greek, meaning 'great bearer', feminine of 'Atlas'.

Atalia: A variant of 'Athalia', meaning 'God's exhaltation'.

Athalia: From the Hebrew, means 'God's exhaltation'.

Athena: From the Greek, meaning 'wise'.

Attie: A variant of 'Athena', meaning 'wise'.

Aubine: French for 'Albinia', meaning 'blond'.

Audrey: From the Anglo Saxon 'Aetheldreda', meaning 'mighty and strong'.

Audry: A variant of 'Audrey', meaning 'mighty and strong'.

Augusta: A feminine form of 'Augustus', meaning 'Majestic'.

Aurelia: From the Latin, meaning 'golden'.

Aurélie: French for 'Aurelia', meaning 'golden'.

Aurora: From the Latin, meaning 'dawn'.

Ava: From the Latin, meaning 'birdlike'.

Aveline: French for 'Hazel', meaning 'like the hazel tree'.

Averil: From the Anglo Saxon, meaning a 'warrior maid'.

Avice: From the French, meaning 'quick tempered'.

Avril: French for 'April', meaning 'warrior maid'.

Babe: A variant of 'Babette' and 'Barbara'.

Babette: A variant of 'Barbara', meaning a 'foreigner'.

Babs: A variant of 'Barbara', meaning a 'foreigner'.

Baptista: From the Latin 'Baptista', meaning 'the Baptiser'.

Barbara: From the Greek, meaning a 'foreigner'.

Barbe: French for 'Barbara', meaning a 'foreigner'.

Bathilda: From the Teutonic, meaning a 'battle maid'.

Bathilde: French for 'Bathilda', meaning 'battle maid'.

Bathsheba: From the Hebrew, meaning the 'seventh daughter'. Bathsheba was the wife of King David.

Bea: A variant of 'Beatrice', meaning a 'bringer of blessings'.

Beatrice: From the Latin, meaning a 'bringer of blessings'.

Beatrix: Spanish and German for 'Beatrice', meaning a 'bringer of blessings'. Example: *Beatrix Potter*.

Beattie: A variant of 'Beatrice', meaning a 'bringer of blessings'.

Becky: A form of 'Rebecca', meaning 'one who is bound'. Example: *Becky Sharp*.

Beda: From the old English, meaning 'maid of war'.

Belinda: From the Italian, meaning 'beautiful serpent'.

Variants are *Bel* and *Linda*.

Belita: Spanish for 'Elizabeth', means 'God's consecrated'.

Belle and **Bella:** Diminutives of 'Isabel' and 'Isabella', 'Arabella' and 'Annabella'.

Bellita: A variant of 'Belle', meaning 'beautiful'.

Benedetta: Italian for 'Benedicta', meaning 'blessed'.

Benedicta: A feminine form of 'Benedict'. From the Latin, meaning 'blessed'.

Benedikta: German for 'Benedicta', meaning 'blessed'.

Benita: A variant of 'Benedicta', meaning 'blessed'.

Benoite: French for 'Benedicta', meaning 'blessed'.

Berenice: From the Greek, meaning 'brings victory'.

Bernadette: From the French, meaning 'brave as a little bear'. Feminine form of 'Bernard'.

Bernadine: A variant of 'Bernadette'.

Bernardina: Spanish and Italian for 'Bernadette'.

Bernice: From the Greek, meaning 'one who brings victory'.

Bernie: A variant of 'Bernice', meaning 'one who brings victory'.

Bertha: From the German, meaning 'bright'.

Berthe: French and German for 'Bertha', meaning 'bright'.

Beryl: From the Greek, meaning a 'jewel'.

Bess and **Bessie:** Variants of 'Elizabeth', meaning 'God's consecrated'.

Beth: A variant of 'Elizabeth'.

Bethan: A traditional Welsh girls' name.

Betsy: A variant of 'Elizabeth'.

Bette: From 'Bertha' and 'Elizabeth'.

Bettina: A variant of 'Elizabeth'.

Beulah: From the Hebrew, meaning 'married'.

Beverley: From this surname, and meaning 'one who dwells at the beaver meadow'.

Bianca: Italian for 'Blanche', meaning 'white'.

Biddy: A form of 'Bridget', meaning 'tall and strong'.

Billie: A form of 'Wilhelmina', meaning 'strong protector'.

Binnie: A variant of 'Benedicta', meaning 'blessed'.

Birdie: A variant of 'Bridget', meaning 'strong'.

Blaise: From the Latin, meaning a 'stammerer'.

Blanca: Spanish for 'Blanche', meaning 'white'.

Blanche: From the French, meaning 'white'.

Blanka: German for 'Blanche', meaning 'white'.

Blossom: Meaning 'like a blossom'.

Bobette: A variant of 'Roberta'.

Bonnie: Meaning 'one who is good'.

Brenda: From the German, meaning a 'flaming sword'.

Bridget: From the Irish, meaning 'strong'.

Bridie: A form of 'Bridget', meaning 'strong'.

Brigida: Spanish and Italian for 'Bridget', meaning 'strong'.

Brigitte: German and French for 'Bridget', meaning 'strong'.

Bronwen: From the Welsh, meaning 'raven haired'.

Brunhilda: From the old German meaning 'warrior maid'.

Bunny: A form of 'Bernice', meaning 'one who brings victory'.

Cäcilia: German for 'Cecilia', meaning 'blind one'.

Cadence: From the Latin, meaning 'one who is rhythmic'.

Cadenza: Italian for 'Cadence', meaning 'one who is rhythmic'.

Calandra: From the Greek, meaning a 'lark'.

Calandre: French for 'Calandra', meaning a 'lark'.

Calandria: Spanish for 'Calandra', meaning a 'lark'.

Calantha: From the Greek, meaning a 'fair blossom'.

Calanthe: French for 'Calantha', meaning a 'fair blossom'.

Calliope: From the Greek, meaning 'one with a lovely voice'.

Camila: Spanish for 'Camille', meaning a 'noble maid'.

Camilla: Italian for 'Camille', meaning a 'noble maid'.

Camille: From the Latin, meaning a 'noble maid'.

Candace: From the Greek, meaning 'of unblemished character'.

Candice: A variant of 'Candace'.

Candida: From the Latin, meaning 'of brilliant whiteness'.

Candide: French for 'Candida', meaning 'of brilliant whiteness'.

Candy: A variant of 'Candace'.

Cara: From the Celtic, meaning a 'friend'.

Carina: A variant of 'Cara', meaning a 'friend'.

Carissa: From the Latin, meaning 'dear one'.

Carla: A variant of 'Charlotte'.

Carlota: Spanish for 'Charlotte'.

Carlotta: Italian for 'Charlotte'.

Carmel: From the Hebrew, meaning 'garden'.

Carmela: Italian for 'Carmel', meaning a 'garden'.

Carmelita: Spanish for 'Carmel', meaning a 'garden'.

Carmen: From the Latin, meaning a 'song', and from the Spanish meaning 'crimson'.

Carmencita: Spanish for 'Carmen', meaning 'crimson'.

Carol and **Carole:** Variants of 'Caroline', meaning 'womanly'.

Carolina: Spanish and Italian for 'Caroline', meaning 'womanly'.

Caroline: From the Latin, meaning 'womanly'.

Carrie: A variant of 'Carol' and 'Caroline'.

Cassandra: From the Greek, meaning 'man's helpmate'.

Cassie: A variant of 'Cassandra', meaning 'man's helpmate'.

Catalina: Spanish for 'Catherine', meaning 'pure'.

Catarina: Italian for 'Catherine', meaning 'pure'.

Catherine: From the Greek, meaning 'pure'. Variants are *Catharine, Cathy, Cath, Kate, Kitty.* Example: *Catherine the Great.*

Cathlene: A variant of 'Catherine'.

Catriona: Scottish for 'Catherine', meaning 'pure'.

Cecile: French for 'Cecilia', meaning 'blind one'.

Cecilia: From the Latin, meaning 'blind one'. Variants are *Celia* and *Cissy*. St Cecilia was a saint in the 3rd century.

Cecily: A variant of 'Cecilia', meaning 'blind one'.

Celeste: From the Latin, meaning 'heavenly'.

Celia: A form of 'Cecilia', meaning 'blind one'.

Charis: A variant of 'Charissa', meaning 'grace'.

Charissa: From the Greek, meaning 'grace'.

Charity: From the Latin 'Charitas', meaning 'charitable'.

Charlene: A variant of 'Charlotte'.

Charlotta: Swedish for 'Charlotte', meaning 'little woman'.

Charlotte: From the French, meaning 'little woman'.

Charmain: A variant of 'Charmaine', meaning a 'singer'.

Charmaine: From the Latin, meaning a 'singer'.

Charyl: A feminine form of 'Charles'.

Cherry: A variant of 'Charity', meaning 'charitable'.

Cheryl: A variant of 'Charlotte', meaning 'little woman'.

Chiara: Italian for 'Clara', meaning 'renowned'.

Chiquita: From the Spanish, meaning 'little one'.

Chlöe: From the Greek, meaning 'young'.

Chris and **Chriss:** Variants of 'Christine'.

Chrissie: A variant of 'Christine', meaning 'follower of Christ'.

Christabel: Means a 'beautiful Christian'.

Christiana: A variant of 'Christine', meaning 'Christian'.

Christine: A feminine form of 'Christian', meaning a 'follower of Christ'. A variant is *Christina.*

Chrystal: A variant of 'Crystal', meaning 'clear as crystal'.

Cicely: A variant of 'Cecilia', meaning 'blind one'.

Cinderella: Means 'from the ashes'. Variants are *Cindy* and *Ella.*

Cis and **Cissie:** Variants of 'Cecilia', meaning 'blind one'.

Claire: French for 'Clara', meaning 'renowned'.

Clara: Means 'renowned'.

Clarabel and **Claribel:** Variants of 'Claire', meaning 'renowned'.

Clarice: From the Latin 'Clarus', meaning 'renowned'.

Clarinda: A variant of 'Clara', meaning 'renowned'.

Clarissa: From the Latin, meaning 'renowned'.

Clarita: Spanish for 'Clara', meaning 'renowned'.

Clarrie: A variant of 'Clara', meaning 'renowned'.

Clary: A variant of 'Clara', meaning 'renowned'.

Claudette: A variant of 'Claudine', meaning 'one who is lame'.

Claudia: From the Latin, meaning 'one who is lame'.

Claudine: French for 'Claudia', meaning 'one who is lame'.

Clemence: French for 'Clementia', meaning 'merciful'.

Clemency: A variant of 'Clemence', meaning 'merciful'.

Clementia: From the Latin, meaning 'merciful'.

Clementina: From the Latin, meaning 'merciful'.

Clementine: From the Latin, meaning 'merciful'.

Cleo: A diminutive of 'Cleopatra', meaning 'fame and glory'.

Cleopatra: From the Greek, meaning 'fame and glory'. Variants are *Cleo* and *Clio*. Cleopatra was Queen of Egypt from 69–30 B.C.

Clodagh: From a stream in Ireland of this name.

Clorinda: From the Latin, meaning 'renowned'.

Clotilde and **Clothilda:** From the German, meaning 'renowned in battle'.

Colleen: From the Irish, meaning 'maiden'.

Colette: A shortened form of the French name 'Nicolette' (a feminine form of 'Nicholas').

Colombe: French for 'Columba', meaning a 'dove'.

Columba: From the Latin, meaning a 'dove'.

Columbine: From the Latin, meaning a 'dove'.

Concepcion: From the Latin, meaning the 'beginning'.

Conchita: Spanish for 'Concepcion', meaning the 'beginning'.

Connie: A variant of 'Constance', meaning 'constant'.

Constance: From the Latin 'Constantia', meaning 'constant'. A daughter of William the Conqueror was named Constance. Variants are Con and Connie.

Constanta: A variant of 'Constance', meaning 'constant'.

Constantia: A variant of 'Constance', meaning 'constant'.

Constanza: Spanish and Italian for 'Constance', meaning 'constant'.

Consuela: Spanish, and meaning 'consolation'.

Consuelo: Italian for 'Consuela', meaning 'consolation'.

Cora: From Greek, meaning a 'maiden'.

Coral: From the Latin, meaning 'under the sea'.

Coralie: French for 'Coral', meaning 'under the sea'.

Cordelia: From the Celtic, meaning 'sea find'. A daughter of King Lear (Shakespeare) was so named. Variants are Della and Delia.

Cordelie: A variant of 'Cordelia', meaning 'sea find'.

Corina: Spanish for 'Cora', meaning a 'maiden'.

Corinna: From the Greek, meaning a 'maiden'.

Corinne: A variant of 'Cora', meaning a 'maiden'.

Cornelia: From the Latin, meaning 'horn-like'.

Cornelie: French for 'Cornelia', meaning 'horn-like'.

Cornelle: A variant of 'Cornelia', meaning 'horn-like'.

Corrie: A variant of 'Cora', meaning a 'maiden'.

Cressida: From the Latin, meaning 'crystal'.

Crispina: The feminine form of 'Crispin'.

Cristina: Spanish and Italian for 'Christine', meaning a 'Christian'.

Crystal: From the Latin, meaning 'clear as crystal'.

Cynthia: From the Greek, meaning the 'moon'.

Daffodil: From the flower so named.

Dahlia: From this flower name.

Daisy: From this flower, and meaning 'day's eye'.

Dana: Meaning 'one who came from Denmark'.

Daniela: From the Hebrew, meaning 'God is my judge'.

Danielle: From the Hebrew, meaning 'God is my judge'. A feminine form of 'Daniel'.

Daphne: From the Greek for 'laurel'.

Darrelle: From the French, meaning 'little and beloved'.

Darryl: As 'Darrelle'.

Davida: Feminine form of 'David', meaning 'beloved'.

Davina: A variant of 'Davida'.

Dawn: Meaning 'of the dawn'. Example: *Dawn Addams*.

Deane: A variant of 'Dena'.

Deanna: A variant of 'Diana', meaning 'goddess'.

Deb and **Debbie:** Variants of 'Deborah'.

Deborah: From the Semitic, meaning 'able'. Example: *Deborah Kerr*.

Debra: A variant of 'Deborah'.

Dee: Used as a variant of 'Deborah'.

Deirdre: From the Gaelic, meaning 'sorrowful'.

Delfine: From the Greek, meaning 'larkspur'.

Delia: From the Greek, meaning 'to be seen'.

Delicia: From the Latin, meaning 'of great delight'.

Delila: A variant of 'Delilah'.

Delilah: Meaning 'delicate'. Delilah was the betrayer of Samson in the Bible (Judges 16.4).

Della: A variant of 'Adelaide'.

Delphine: As 'Delfine'.

Demetria: From the Greek 'Demeter', the goddess of the harvest.

Dena: Meaning 'one who lives in a valley'.

Denise: From 'Dionysius', the Greek god of wine.

Desdemona: From the Greek, meaning 'ill fated one'.

Desiree: From the French, meaning 'one desired'.

Diana: Meaning 'goddess'. Diana of the Ephesians is mentioned in the Bible in Acts 19.28. Variants are *Di* and *Deanna*.

Diane: As 'Diana'.

Dianna: A variant of 'Diana'.

Dilys: Meaning 'sure' or 'constant'.

Dinah: From the Hebrew, meaning 'judged'. Dinah was a daughter of Jacob (Genesis 30.2). Variants are *Di* and *Dina*.

Dixie: A variant of 'Benedicta'.

Dodo: A form of 'Dorothy'.

Doll and **Dolly:** Forms of 'Dorothy'.

Dolores: From the Spanish, meaning 'sorrowful'.

Dominga: Spanish for 'Dominica'.

Dominica: Meaning 'of the Lord'.

Dominique: French for 'Dominica'.

Doña: Spanish for 'Donna'.

Donna: From the Italian, meaning a 'lady'.

Dora: From the Greek, meaning a 'gift'. A variant is Dorrie.

Dorcas: Means a 'gazelle'. In the Bible Dorcas was raised from the dead by Peter (Acts 9.40).

Doreen: A variant of 'Dora'.

Doretta: A variant of 'Dora', meaning 'a gift'.

Dorinda: From the Greek, meaning a 'lovely gift'.

Doris: Meaning a 'girl of the Ancient Greek place named Doria'. A variant is Dorrie.

Dorotea: Spanish and Italian for 'Dorothy'.

Dorothea: From the Greek, meaning 'gift of God'. German for 'Dorothy'.

Dorothy: As 'Dorothea'.

Dorrie: A variant of 'Dora'.

Dorthée: French for 'Dorothy'.

Dot: A variant of 'Dorothy'.

Doxie: From the Greek, meaning 'of good report'.

Drusie: A variant of 'Drusilla'.

Drusilla: From the Latin, meaning 'of the family of Drusus'. Mentioned in Acts 24.24

Duana: From the Irish Gaelic, meaning 'little dark girl'.

Dulcie: From the Latin, meaning 'sweet one'.

Eilidh

Eartha: From the old English, meaning 'of the earth'.

Ebba: An old English variant of 'Eve'.

Eda: From the old English 'Eada' meaning 'blessed'.

Edie: A variant of 'Edith'.

Edita: Italian for 'Edith'.

Edith: From the Anglo Saxon 'Eadgyth', meaning 'prosperous'. Variants are Ede and Edie.

Ediva: The wife of Edward the Confessor was so named. A variant of 'Edith'.

Edmunda: A feminine form of 'Edmund'.

Edna: From the Hebrew, meaning 'reborn'.

Edwina: Feminine form of 'Edward'.

Effie: A variant of 'Euphemia'.

Eileen: From the Irish, meaning 'light'.

Elaine: From the French 'Helene', meaning 'light'.

Elberta: A variant of 'Alberta'.

Eldrida: From the old English, meaning 'wise'.

Eleanor(e): From the French 'Helene', meaning 'light'. Variants are Ella, Ellie, Nell, Nellie.

Eleanora: Italian for 'Eleanor'.

Eleanore: Danish and German for 'Eleanor'.

Electra: From the Greek, meaning 'light one'. Electra was the daughter of Atlas.

Elena: Italian for 'Helen', meaning 'light'.

Elga: From the Norse, meaning 'holy'.

Elinor(e): A variant of 'Eleanor'.

Elisa: Italian for 'Elizabeth'.

Elisabet: Swedish for 'Elizabeth'.

Elsie: A variant of 'Elizabeth' and 'Elisabeth'.

Elizabeth: From the Hebrew, meaning 'God's oath'. Variants are *Liz, Lissie, Eliza, Beth, Bet, Betty, Libby, Betsey, Liza* and *Lissa*. Example: *Elizabeth Browning.*

Ella: From the Anglo Saxon, meaning 'elf-like'. Example: *Ella Fitzgerald.*

Ellen: From the French 'Helene', meaning 'light'. Example: *Ellen Terry.*

Ellice: Feminine of 'Ellis', q.v.

Elma: From the Greek, meaning 'pleasant'.

Eloise: A variant of 'Louise', meaning a 'warrior maid'.

Elsa: From the Teutonic, meaning 'noble'.

Else: Dutch, Danish and German for 'Elizabeth'.

Elsie: From the Teutonic, meaning 'noble'.

Elspeth: Scottish form of 'Elizabeth'.

Elvina: From the Anglo Saxon, meaning 'friend of the elf'.

Elvira: From the Latin, meaning 'blond one'.

Elvire: French for 'Elvira'.

Elysia: From the Latin, meaning 'blissful'.

Ema: Spanish for 'Emma'.

Emeline: A variant of 'Amelia'.

Emilia: Spanish, Dutch and Italian for 'Emily'.

Emilie: French for 'Emily'.

Emily: From the Latin, meaning 'winning'. Example: *Emily Brönte*.

Emma: From the Teutonic, meaning 'of the universe'. Variants are *Em* and *Emmie*.

Ena: From the Gaelic, meaning 'fiery'.

Engelberta: A feminine form of 'Engelbert'.

Engracia: Spanish for 'Grace'.

Enid: From the Celtic, meaning 'pure'.

Enrichetta: Italian for 'Henrietta'.

Enriqueta: Spanish for 'Henrietta'.

Erica: A feminine form of 'Eric'.

Erika: Swedish for 'Erica'.

Erma: From the Teutonic, meaning 'noble maid'.

Ermintrude: From the Teutonic, meaning 'mighty and beloved'.

Ernestine: A feminine form of 'Ernest'.

Esme: A diminutive of 'Esmeralda'.

Esmeralda: Spanish for 'this gem'.

Estelle: From the Latin 'Stella', meaning a 'star'.

Ester: Spanish and Italian for 'Esther'.

Esther: From the Hebrew, meaning a 'star'. Variants are *Essie* and *Ettie*.

Estrella: Spanish for 'Estelle'.

Ethel: From the Anglo Saxon 'Aethel', meaning 'noble'.

Etta and **Ettie:** Variants of 'Henrietta'.

Eufemia: Spanish and Italian for 'Euphemia'.

Eugenia: From the Greek, meaning 'noble'.

Eugenie: A variant of 'Eugenia'.

Eunice: From the Greek, meaning 'victory'.

Euphemia: From the Greek, meaning 'well spoken'. A variant is *Effie*.

Eva: As 'Eve'.

Evadne: From the Greek, meaning 'high born'.

Evangeline: From the Greek, meaning 'bearer of good news'. Example: *Evangeline Booth*.

Eve: From the Hebrew, meaning 'life giver'.

Evelyn: A variant of 'Eve'.

Faith: From the Anglo Saxon, meaning a 'believer in God'.

Fanny: A form of 'Frances'. Example: *Fanny Burney*.

Faustina: Italian for 'Faustine'.

Faustine: From the Latin, meaning 'lucky'.

Fay: From 'Faith', meaning a 'believer in God'.

Federica: Italian for 'Frederica'.

Fedora: Russian for 'Theodora'.

Felice and **Felicia:** From the Latin, meaning 'lucky'.

Felicidad: Spanish for 'Felice'.

Felicie: French for 'Felice'.

Felicity: From the Latin, meaning 'lucky'.

Felipa: Spanish for 'Philippa'.

Fenella: From the Gaelic, meaning 'of the white shoulders'.

Feodosia: Russian for 'Theodosia'.

Fifi: French for 'Josephine'.

Filide: Italian for 'Phyllis'.

Filippa: Italian for 'Philippa'.

Fiona: From the Irish, meaning 'fair one'.

Fiora: Italian for 'Flora'.

Fiorenza: Italian for 'Florence'.

Flavia: From the Latin, meaning 'flaxen haired'.

Fleur: From the French for 'flower'.

Fleurette: A variant of 'Fleur'.

Flor: Spanish for 'Flora'.

Flora: From the Latin, meaning 'flower'. A variant is 'Flo'.

Flore: French for 'Flora'.

Florence: From the Latin, meaning 'flourishing'. Example: *Florence Nightingale*.

Florencia: Spanish for 'Florence'.

Florentia: German for 'Florence'.

Floris: A variant of 'Florence'.

Florrie: A variant of 'Florence'.

Flossie: A variant of 'Florence'.

Frances: From the Latin, meaning 'free'. Variants are *Fanny* and *Fan*.

Francesca: Italian for 'Frances'.

Francisca: Spanish for 'Frances'.

Franziska: German for 'Frances'.

Freda: From the Teutonic, meaning 'peaceful'.

Frederica: From the Teutonic, meaning 'peaceful ruler'.

Frédérique: French for 'Frederica'.

Freya: From the name of a Norse goddess.

Friederike: German for 'Frederica'.

Fulvia: From the Latin, meaning 'of the yellow hair'.

Gabrielle: From the Hebrew, meaning 'of God'. A feminine form of 'Gabriel'. A variant is *Gabby*.

Gail: A diminutive of 'Abigail', meaning 'joy of my Father'.

Galatea: From the Greek, meaning 'white as milk'.

Gale: A variant of 'Gail'.

Gay: Meaning the 'gay one'.

Gaynor: From 'Guinevere', meaning 'white and noble'. Guinevere was the wife of King Arthur.

Gazella: Meaning 'like a gazelle'.

Gemma: From the Italian, meaning a 'gem'.

Gene: A variant of 'Eugenia', meaning 'of noble birth'. Example: *Gene Stratton Porter*.

Genevieve: From the Celtic, meaning 'white and noble'.

Georgette: French for 'Georgia'.

Georgia: A feminine form of 'George'.

Georgina: German and Dutch for 'Georgia'.

Geraldine: A feminine form of 'Gerald', meaning 'ruler with a spear'.

Gerda: From the Norse, meaning 'shielded'.

Gerhardine: German for 'Geraldine'.

Germaine: From the German, meaning 'of Germany'.

Gertrud: German for 'Gertrude'.

Gertruda: Italian for 'Gertrude'.

Gertrude: From the Teutonic, meaning 'of the beloved spear'. Variants are *Gert* and *Gertie*.

Gertrudis: Spanish for 'Gertrude'.

Gida: Countess Gida is mentioned in the Domesday book (11th century). The name means 'protected'.

Gilda: From the old English, meaning 'golden'.

Gillian: From 'Juliana', meaning a 'young one'. Variants are *Gill* and *Jill*.

Gilly: A variant of 'Gillian', and also Cornish for a 'grove'.

Gina: From 'Regina', meaning a 'queen'.

Ginger: One who is auburn haired.

Giorgia: Italian for 'Georgia'.

Giovanna: Italian for 'Jane'.

Giralda: Italian for 'Geraldine'.

Gisela: Spanish and Italian for 'Giselle'.

Gisele: French for 'Giselle'.

Giselle: From the Teutonic, meaning a 'hostage'.

Gitana: From the Spanish, meaning a 'gypsy'.

Giuditta: Italian for 'Judith'.

Giuletta: Italian for 'Julia'.

Giustina: Italian for 'Justine'.

Gladys: From the Celtic, and meaning 'one who limps'.

Glenda: From the Celtic, and meaning 'one who dwells in the glen'.

Glenna: As 'Glenda'.

Gloria: From the Latin 'Gloria', meaning 'glorious'. A variant is Glory.

Gloriana: A variant of 'Gloria'.

Glynis: From the Celtic, meaning a 'glen dweller'.

Goda: A little known Christian name seldom used today, but this name is mentioned in the Domesday book (11th century) and means 'God's gift'.

Godiva: From the Anglo Saxon, meaning 'God's gift'. Lady Godiva - the wife of Leofric - is said to have ridden round naked on horse back in the streets of Coventry.

Goida: From the Hebrew, meaning 'golden'.

Goldie: From the Anglo Saxon, meaning 'golden haired'.

Grace: From the Latin 'Gratia', meaning 'grace and thanks'.

Grazia: Italian for 'Grace'.

Greer: A variant of 'Gregoria'. Example: Greer Garson.

Gregoria: A feminine form of 'Gregory', meaning 'watchful'.

Greta: A variant of 'Margaret'.

Gretal: German for 'Margaret'.

Gretchen: German for 'Margaret'.

Griselda: From the German, meaning 'battle maid'.

Grishilde: Dutch and German for 'Griselda'.

Grizzel: A variant of 'Griselda' and mentioned in the Somerset House records of 1905.

Gueda: From the Anglo Saxon, meaning 'good'. This name is mentioned in the Domesday book (11th century).

Guglielma: Italian for 'Wilhelmina'.

Guida: From the Italian, meaning a 'teacher'.

Guillelmina: Spanish for 'Wilhelmina'.

Guillelmine: French for 'Wilhelmina'.

Guinevere: Meaning 'white and noble'. Guinevere was the wife of King Arthur.

Gunhilda: From the German, meaning 'war maid'.

Gwenda: As 'Gwendolen'.

Gwendolen: From the Celtic, meaning 'white or fair haired'. A variant is *Gwen*.

Gwynneth: From the Celtic, meaning 'fair haired'.

Hagar: From the Hebrew, meaning 'forsaken'.

Haidee: From the Greek, meaning 'modest'.

Hannah: From the Hebrew, meaning 'graceful'. Variants are *Nan* and *Anna*. Hannah was the mother of Samuel.

Harmony: From the Latin 'Harmonia', meaning 'concord'.

Harriet: From the French 'Henrietta', meaning 'ruler of the home'. Example: *Harriet Beecher Stowe*.

Hattie: A variant of 'Henrietta'. A variant is *Hatty*.

Hayley: Meaning 'one who lived originally by a "Hay Lea"' (e.g. a meadow).

Hazel: From the Anglo Saxon, meaning 'like the hazel tree'.

Heather: From the Anglo Saxon, meaning 'as the heather'.

Hebe: From the Greek, meaning 'youth'. In Greek mythology Hebe was the daughter of Zeus.

Hedda: From the Teutonic, meaning 'strife'.

Hedwig: From the German, meaning 'strife'.

Hedy: From the Greek, meaning 'pleasant'.

Heidi: As 'Hedda'.

Helen: From the Greek, meaning 'light'. Variants are *Nell, Nellie* and *Lena*. Examples: *Helen of Troy* and *Helen Keller*.

Helena: As 'Helen'.

Helene: German for 'Helen', meaning 'light'.

Hélène: French for 'Helen'.

Helga: From the Norse, meaning 'holy'.

Helma: From the Teutonic, meaning 'protection'.

Heloise: From the Teutonic, meaning 'healthy'.

Hendricka: A variant of 'Henrika' and a name mentioned in the records at Somerset House in 1904.

Hendrika: Dutch for 'Henrietta'.

Henrietta: From the French 'Henriette', meaning 'ruler of the home'. Variants are *Hetty, Hattie, Etta, Netta* and *Netty*. Henrietta was the wife of King Charles the First.

Henrika: A variant of 'Henrietta'.

Hermia: From the Greek, meaning 'of the earth'.

Hermione: From the Greek, meaning 'of the earth'.

Hertha: From the Anglo Saxon, meaning 'of the earth'. A variant is *Eartha*.

Hester: From the Greek, meaning a 'star'.

Hilary: From the Latin, meaning 'cheerful'.

Hilda: From the Teutonic, meaning 'battle maid'.

Hildegard: From the Teutonic, meaning 'strong in battle'.

Holly: From the Anglo Saxon, meaning 'holly'.

Honey: From the Anglo Saxon, meaning 'sweet'.

Honor: From the Latin, meaning 'one of honour'.

Honoria: From the Latin, meaning 'one of honour'. Variants are *Nora* and *Honor*.

Hope: From the Anglo Saxon, meaning 'one of hope'.

Horatia: From the Latin, meaning 'keeper of the light'. The feminine form of 'Horace'.

Hortense: From the Latin, meaning 'of the garden'.

Hortensia: Dutch, German and Danish for 'Hortense'.

Huberta: The feminine form of 'Hubert', meaning a 'great mind'.

Hyacinth: From the flower of this name. A variant is *Cynthia*.

Hyacinthe: French for 'Hyacinth'.

Hyacinthie: German for 'Hyacinth'.

Hypatia: From the Greek, meaning the 'highest'.

Ida: From the Teutonic, meaning 'prosperous'.

Ileana: From the Greek, meaning 'one from the city of Illium'.

Ilene: A variant of 'Aileen'.

Imogen: From the Latin, meaning a 'lively image'.

Ina: A variant of a number of names ending in 'ina' (particularly used in Scotland), such as 'Georgina', 'Wilhelmina' etc.

Inez: Spanish for 'Agnes'.

Inga: A Scandinavian variant of 'Ingrid'.

Ingrid: From the Norse, meaning 'daughter of a hero'.

Iolanthe: From the Greek, meaning 'violet'. Iolanthe is the chief character in one of Gilbert and Sullivan's light operas.

Iphigenia: From the Greek, meaning 'strong'.

Irene: From the Greek, meaning 'peace'. A variant is Rene.

Iris: From the Greek meaning 'rainbow'.

Irma: From the German, meaning 'noble one'.

Isa: A diminutive of 'Isabel'.

Isabeau: French for 'Isabel'.

Isabel: As for 'Isabella'.

Isabella: From the Spanish, meaning 'God's consecrated'.

Isabelle: German for 'Isobel'.

Isadora: The feminine form of 'Isidore'.

Iseult: From the Welsh, meaning 'one who is fair'.

Isis: From the Egyptian, meaning 'goddess supreme'.

Isobel: Scottish form of 'Isabel', meaning 'God's consecrated'.

Isolde: From the Welsh, meaning 'one who is fair'.

Ivy: From the Anglo Saxon, and from the plant of this name.

Jacinta: Spanish for 'Hyacinth'.

Jacintha: From the Greek, meaning 'like a hyacinth'.

Jacinthe: A variant of 'Jacintha'.

Jackie: A variant of 'Jacqueline'.

Jacqueline: From the French, meaning 'one who supplants'. A feminine form of 'Jacques'.

Jacquetta: A variant of 'Jacqueline'.

Jamesina: In Scotland where the family wanted a son, and a daughter is born, it is customary to add 'ina' onto a masculine name. The owners of these names are usually referred to as 'Ina', and not by their full name.

Jan: A diminutive of 'Janet'.

Jane: From the Hebrew, meaning 'God is gracious'.

Janet and **Janette:** Variants of 'Jane'.

Janice: A variant of 'Jane'.

Jasmin and **Jasmine:** From the Persian, and meaning 'like the Jasmine'.

Jayne: A variant of 'Jane'.

Jean: From the French, meaning 'God is gracious'. Scottish form of 'Jane'. A variant is *Jeannie*.

Jeanette: French for 'Jane'.

Jem: A diminutive of 'Jemima'.

Jemima: From the Hebrew, meaning a 'dove'. Variants are *Jem* and *Mima*. One of the daughters of Job was named Jemima.

Jennifer: A variant of 'Guinevere'. Variants are *Jennie* and *Jenny*.

Jenny: A variant of 'Jennifer'. Example: *Jenny Lind*.

Jess and **Jessie:** Variants of 'Jessica'.

Jessamine: As 'Jasmine'.

Jessica: From the Hebrew, meaning 'one who is wealthy'. Variants are *Jess* and *Jessie*. Jessica was the daughter of Shylock in Shakespeare's 'Merchant of Venice'.

Jewel: Meaning 'one who is a jewel'.

Jill: A diminutive of 'Jillian' and 'Gillian'.

Jinnie: A variant of 'Jane'.

Jo: A diminutive of 'Josephine'.

Joan: From the Hebrew, meaning 'God is gracious'.

Joanna and **Joanne:** As 'Joan'.

Jocelyn: From the old English, meaning a 'just one'. Variants are *Joscelin* and *Joselin*.

Johanna: German for 'Jane'.

Jose: A variant of 'Josephine'.

Josefa: Spanish for 'Josephine'.

Josepha: German for 'Josephine'.

Josephine: From the Hebrew, meaning 'he shall increase'.

Josette: A variant of 'Josephine'.

Josie: A variant of 'Josephine'.

Joy: Meaning 'one who is joyful'.

Joyce: From the French 'Joyeuse', meaning 'merry'.

Juanita: Spanish for 'Jane'.

Judith: From the Hebrew, meaning 'to be praised'. A variant is Judy.

Judy: See 'Judith'.

Julia: Meaning 'young'. Often given to those born in July.

Juliana: A variant of 'Julia'.

Julie: German for 'Julia'.

Juliet: A variant of Julia.

Julieta: Spanish for 'Julia'.

Juliette: French for 'Julia'.

June: A name usually given to those who were born in the month of June.

Juno: From the Latin, meaning 'of the heavens'. Juno was a mythical Roman goddess.

Justina: Spanish for 'Justine'.

Justine: A feminine form of 'Justus', meaning 'just'.

Karen: Dutch for 'Katherine'.

Karlotte: German for 'Charlotte'.

Karoline: German for 'Caroline'.

Kate: A diminutive of 'Katherine'.

Katherine: From the Greek, meaning 'pure'. Variants are *Kitty, Kit, Katharine, Kathie, Kath, Kate, Katie.*

Kathleen: Irish for 'Katherine'.

Katie: A variant of 'Katherine'.

Katinka: Russian for 'Catherine'.

Kay: A variant of 'Katherine'.

Keira: From the Celtic, meaning 'black haired'.

Kelly: From the Irish Gaelic, meaning 'warrior maiden'.

Kim: From the Anglo Saxon, meaning 'one who rules'.

Kirsten: Scandinavian for 'Christine'.

Kirstin: The Scottish form of 'Christina'.

Kirsty: A variant of 'Kirstin'.

Kit and Kitty: Variants of 'Katherine'.

Klara: German for 'Clara'.

Kora: A variant of 'Cora'.

Kristel: German for 'Christine'.

Lalita: From the Sanscrit, meaning 'free of guile'.

Lana: From the Gaelic, meaning 'beautiful'.

Lara: Means 'one who is famous'.

Laraine: From the Latin, meaning 'godlike'.

Larissa: From the Greek, meaning 'cheerful'.

Laura: From the Latin, meaning 'of the laurels'. The feminine form of 'Lawrence'.

Laurabel: A name in the records of Somerset House, London (1902), and meaning 'beautiful laurel'.

Laurel: A variant of 'Laura'.

Lauren: From the Latin, and meaning 'of the laurels'.

Lauretta: A name mentioned in the records of Somerset House, London (1905). A variant of 'Laura', and meaning 'laurel crowned'.

Laurette: French for 'Laura'.

Laurie: A variant of 'Laura'.

Lavender: Named after this sweet smelling plant.

Lavina: A variant of 'Lavinia'.

Lavinia: Means 'of Latvium'.

Lea and **Lee:** A variant of 'Leah'.

Leah: From the Hebrew, meaning 'languid'. Variants are *Lea* and *Lee*. The wife of Jacob was named Leah (Genesis 29.26).

Leana: From the French, meaning 'one who clings'.

Leanor: Spanish for 'Eleanore'.

Leanore: A variant of 'Eleanore'.

Leatrice: A variant of 'Beatrice'.

Leda: A variant of 'Alida'.

Leetice: French for 'Letitia'.

Leila: From the Persian, meaning 'dark haired'.

Lela: A variant of 'Leila'.

Lena: A variant of 'Helena', meaning 'light'.

Lenore: From the Greek, meaning 'merciful'.

Leonie: The feminine form of 'Leon', meaning 'like a lion'.

Leonora: The Italian form of 'Eleanora', meaning 'light'.

Lesley: From the Gaelic, meaning 'one who dwells by the pool'.

Leta: A variant of 'Letha'.

Letha: From the Greek, meaning 'forgetting'.

Leticia: Spanish for 'Letitia'.

Letitia: From the Latin, meaning 'joy'.

Letizia: Italian for 'Letitia'.

Lettice: From the Latin, meaning 'joy'.

Liana: From the French, meaning 'one who clings'.

Libby: A variant of 'Elizabeth', meaning 'consecrated by God'.

Lidia: Spanish and Italian for 'Lydia'.

Lila: A variant of 'Lillian'.

Lili: German for 'Lillian'.

Lilias: Scottish for 'Lillian'.

Lilibet: A variant of 'Elizabeth'.

Lilith: Semitic, meaning 'of the night'.

Lilli: A variant of 'Lily'.

Lillian: From the Latin, meaning 'a lily'. (Also spelt 'Lilian').

Lily: From the Latin, meaning 'like a lily'. A variant is *Lil*.

Lina: A variant of 'Caroline' and 'Adeline'.

Linda: From the Spanish, meaning 'pretty'. A variant is *Lindy*.

Lindy: A variant of 'Linda'.

Linette: Meaning 'like a linnet'.

Lis: French for 'Lillian'.

Lisa: A variant of 'Elizabeth'.

Lisabet: A variant of 'Elizabeth'.

Lisbeth: A variant of 'Elisabeth'.

Lisette: French for 'Elizabeth'.

Lissa: A variant of 'Melissa'.

Lita: From 'Carmelita', meaning 'of God's garden'.

Livia: A diminutive of 'Olivia'.

Liz and **Liza:** Variants of 'Elizabeth'. Example: *Liza Doolittle*.

Lois: From 'Louise', meaning a 'warrior maid'.

Lola: A variant of 'Dolores', meaning 'sorrowful'.

Lolita: A variant of 'Dolores', meaning 'sorrowful'.

Lora: A variant of 'Laura'.

Lorelei: The name of the German Rhine maiden who lured sailors to their deaths.

Loren: A variant of 'Laura'.

Lorenza: Italian for 'Laura'.

Loretta: From 'Laura', meaning 'of the laurels'.

Lorita: A variant of 'Laura'.

Lorna: A form of 'Laura', meaning 'of the laurels'. Example:

Lorna Doone of R.H. Blackmore's book with this title.

Lottie: A variant of 'Charlotte'.

Lou: A variant of 'Louise'.

Louella: A combination of 'Louise' and 'Ella'.

Louisa: From the Teutonic, meaning 'warrior maid'. Variants are *Lou, Louie, Lulu*. Example: *Louisa Alcott*.

Louise: From the Teutonic, meaning 'warrior maid'. Variants are *Lou, Louie, Lulu*.

Luce: A variant of 'Lucy'.

Lucia: Italian for 'Lucy'.

Lucienne: French for 'Lucy'.

Lucille: From the Latin, meaning 'light'.

Lucinda: From the Latin, meaning 'light'.

Lucrèce: French for 'Lucretia'.

Lucrecia: Spanish for 'Lucretia'.

Lucretia: From the Latin, 'to gain'. Example: *Lucretia Borgia*.

Lucrezia: Italian for 'Lucretia'.

Lucy: From the Latin, meaning 'light'. A variant is *Lou*.

Luisa: Italian and Spanish for 'Louise'.

Luise: German for 'Louisa'.

Lulu: A variant of 'Louisa', meaning 'warrior maid'.

Luz: Spanish for 'Lucy'.

Lydia: From the Greek, meaning 'woman of Lydia' (Asia Minor). (Acts 16.14).

Lydie: French for 'Lydia'.

Lynette: A variant of 'Linette'.

Lynn: From the Celtic, meaning 'of the pool'.

Lysandra: From the Greek, and the feminine of 'Lysander', meaning a 'liberator'.

Mab: From the Gaelic, meaning 'joyful'. Mab was reputed to have been queen of the fairies.

Mabel: Meaning 'one who is lovable'.

Mabelle: French for 'Mabel'.

Madalena: Spanish for 'Madeline'.

Maddelena: Italian for 'Madeline'.

Madeleine: French for 'Madeline', meaning a 'woman from Magdala' (Palestine). Variants are *Maddie* and *Lina*.

Madeline: Meaning a 'woman from Magdala'.

Madge: A variant of 'Margaret', meaning a 'pearl'.

Mady: German for 'Madeline'.

Mae: A variant of 'May'.

Magda: German for 'Madeline'.

Magdalen: From the Hebrew, meaning a 'woman of Magdala' (Palestine).

Magdalene: German for 'Madeline'. Example: *Mary Magdalene*.

Maggie: A variant of 'Margaret', meaning a 'pearl'.

Magnolia: From the flower name. Variants are *Nola* and *Maggie*.

Maidie and **Maida:** Variants of 'Margaret', meaning a 'pearl'.

Mairi: Scottish for 'Mary', meaning 'bitter'.

Maisie: A Scottish variant of 'Margaret', meaning a 'pearl'.

Mala: A variant of 'Madeline'.

Mame: A variant of 'Mary', meaning 'bitter'.

Mamie: A variant of 'Mary', meaning 'bitter'.

Manda: A diminutive of 'Amanda'.

Mandy: A variant of 'Amanda'.

Manette: French for 'Mary'.

Marcela: Spanish for 'Marcella'.

Marcella: The feminine form of 'Marcellus', meaning 'warlike'. A variant is *Marcy*.

Marcelle: French for 'Marcella'.

Marchita: A variant of 'Marcia'.

Marcia: The feminine form of 'Marcus', meaning 'warlike'.

Marcie: French for 'Marcia'.

Margaret: From the Greek, meaning a 'pearl'. Variants are *Greta, Margie, Maggie, Meg, Peg, Rita, Margo*. Example: *Princess Margaret*.

Margarete: Danish and German for 'Margaret'.

Margaretha: Dutch for 'Margaret'.

Margarita: Spanish for 'Margaret'.

Margherita: Italian for 'Margaret'.

Margo: A variant of Margaret'.

Margot: A variant of 'Margaret', meaning a 'pearl'. Variants are *Margo* and *Margie*.

Marguerite: French form of 'Margaret', meaning a 'pearl'.

Mari: An Irish form of 'Mary', meaning 'bitter'.

Maria: Spanish and Italian for 'Mary'.

Marian: A French variant of 'Marion'.

Mariana: Spanish for 'Marion'.

Marianna: Italian for 'Marion'.

Marianne: German and French for 'Marion'.

Maribella: A combination of 'Mary' and 'Bella'.

Marie: French for 'Mary'. Example: *Marie Antoinette*.

Marigold: From this flower name.

Marilda and **Marelda:** From the Germanic, meaning 'battle maid'.

Marilyn: A variant of 'Mary'.

Marina: From the Latin, meaning 'of the sea'.

Marion: A variant of 'Mary'. Example: *Maid Marion* of Robin Hood fame.

Mariota: A name mentioned in the Hundred Rolls (13th century). A variant of 'Mary', meaning 'bitter'.

Marjorie: A variant of 'Margaret', meaning a 'pearl'. Variants are *Margie* and *Marge*.

Marjory: As 'Marjorie'.

Marlene: German for 'Madeline'.

Marquita: A variant of 'Marcia'.

Marsha: As 'Marcia', meaning 'warlike'.

Marta: Spanish, Swedish and Italian for 'Martha'.

Martha: From the Hebrew, meaning a 'lady'. Variants are *Marta*, *Mattie* and *Mat*. Martha was the sister of Lazarus.

Marthe: French and German for 'Martha'.

Martina: A feminine form of 'Martin', meaning 'warlike'.

Martine: French for 'Martina'.

Martita: A variant of 'Martha'.

Mary: From the Hebrew, meaning 'bitter'. Variants are *Polly*, *Mame*, *Molly* and *Mamie*. Example: *Mary Queen of Scots*.

Maryann: A combination of 'Mary' and 'Ann'.

Marylou: A combination of 'Mary' and 'Louise'.

Matelda: Italian for 'Matilda'.

Mathilde: French for 'Matilda'.

Matilda: From the Teutonic, meaning 'Battle maiden'. Variants are *Mat, Mattie* and *Tilly*. Matilda was the Queen of William the Conqueror (1066).

Matilde: Spanish for 'Matilda'.

Mattie: A variant of 'Martha'.

Maud and **Maude:** From the old Norman French, meaning 'battle maid'.

Maura: From the Irish for 'Mary', meaning 'bitter'.

Maureen: From the Irish, meaning 'little Mary'.

Maurizia: Italian for 'Maureen'.

Mavis: From the French, meaning 'like the song thrush'.

Maxie: A variant of 'Maxine'.

Maxine: From the Latin, meaning 'one of high rank'. A variant is *Maxie*.

May: From the May blossom and the Roman goddess 'Maia'.

Maybelle: Meaning 'beautiful May'.

Meave: Irish for 'Mab'.

Meg: A variant of 'Margaret', meaning a 'pearl'.

Megan: From the Gaelic for 'Margaret', meaning a 'pearl'.

Mehetabel: From the Hebrew, meaning 'happy in God'.

Melanie: From the Greek, meaning 'of dark hair or complexion'.

Melina: Italian for 'Carmel'.

Melinda: From the Latin, meaning 'as sweet as honey'. Variants are *Lindy* and *Linda*.

Melisande: French for 'Millicent'.

Melisenda: Spanish for 'Millicent'.

Melissa: From the Latin, meaning 'honey sweet'. A variant is *Lissa*.

Melody: From the Anglo Saxon, meaning 'one who is melodious'.

Mercedes: : Spanish for 'Mercy'.

Mercy: From the Anglo Saxon, meaning 'compassionate'.

Merle: From the French, meaning 'like a blackbird'.

Michaela: From the Hebrew, meaning 'godlike'. The feminine form of 'Michael'.

Michaella: Italian for 'Michaela'.

Michelle: French for 'Michaela'.

Mickie: A variant of 'Michaela'.

Mignon: From the French, meaning a 'favourite'.

Mignonette: A variant of 'Mignon', meaning a 'favourite'.

Miguelita: Spanish for 'Michaela'.

Mildred: From the German, meaning 'mild counsellor'. Variants are Mil and Milly.

Millicent: From the Teutonic, meaning 'strong and true'. Variants are Mil and Millie.

Mimi: From the Hebrew, meaning 'bitter'. Mimi is the name of the heroine in 'La Boheme'.

Mina: A diminutive of 'Wilhelmina', meaning 'strong protector'.

Minerva: From the Greek, meaning 'one who thinks'.

Minette: French for 'Minerva'.

Minna: From the Teutonic, meaning 'love'.

Minnie: A Scottish form of 'Mary', meaning 'bitter'. A variant is Min.

Mira: A diminutive of 'Mirabel'.

Mirabel: From the Latin, meaning 'wonderful'. Variants are Mira and Myra.

Miranda: From the Latin, meaning 'wonderful'. Variants are Myra and Mira.

Miriam: From the Hebrew, meaning 'bitter'. A variant is *Mitzi*.

Mitzi: A variant of 'Miriam', meaning 'bitter'.

Modesta: Italian for 'Modesty'.

Modestia: Spanish for 'Modesty'.

Modestine: French for 'Modesty'.

Modesty: From the Latin, meaning 'modest'.

Moira: Irish for 'Mary', meaning 'bitter'.

Moireen: A variant of 'Maureen'.

Molly: A variant of 'Mary', meaning 'bitter'. Variants are *Moll* and *Mollie*. Example: *Molly Malone*.

Mona: From the Gaelic, meaning a 'noble lady'.

Monica: From the Greek, meaning 'one alone'.

Morag: Scottish for 'Sarah'.

Morena: Spanish for 'Maureen'.

Morgana: From the Welsh, meaning 'of the sea shore'.

Moyna: A variant of 'Myrna'.

Muriel: From the Celtic, meaning 'from the bright sea'.

Myfanwy: From the Welsh, meaning 'water maiden'.

Myra: From the Latin, meaning 'wonderful'.

Myrna: From the Gaelic, meaning 'gentle'.

Myrtle: From the Greek, meaning 'like the myrtle'.

Nadine: From the Russian, meaning 'hope'.

Nan: A variant of 'Anne', meaning 'grace'.

Nana: A variant of 'Hannah'.

Nancy: A variant of 'Anne', meaning 'grace'.

Nanette: A variant of 'Anne', meaning 'grace'.

Naomi: From the Hebrew, meaning 'delightful one'.

Natalia: Spanish for 'Natalie'.

Natalie: From the Latin, meaning 'birthday'. Variants are *Netta* and *Nettie*.

Natasha: Russian for 'Natalie'.

Nathania: Feminine of 'Nathan'.

Nell and **Nellie:** Variants of 'Ellen' and 'Helen', meaning 'bright'. Examples: *Nell Gwyn* and *Nellie Melba*.

Nella: A variant of 'Cornelia'.

Nerice: A variant of 'Nerine'.

Nerine: From the Greek, meaning 'from the sea'.

Nerissa: A variant of 'Nerine'.

Nessa: A variant of 'Nessie' and 'Agnes'.

Nessie: A variant of 'Agnes', meaning 'pure'. Nessie is the name of the 'Loch Ness Monster'.

Nesta: Welsh for 'Agnes'.

Netta and **Nettie:** Variants of 'Henrietta', meaning 'ruler of the home'.

Nicola: A variant of 'Nicole'.

Nicole: From the Greek, meaning 'victorious'. The feminine form of 'Nicholas'. Variants are *Nikki* and *Nicky*.

Nicolette: A feminine form of 'Nicholas'.

Nikki: A variant of 'Nicole'.

Nina: From the Spanish, meaning a 'girl'.

Ninette: A variant of 'Nina'.

Nita: A variant of 'Anita' and 'Juanita'.

Noelle: French for 'Natalie'.

Nola: From the Gaelic, meaning 'famous'.

Nona: From the Latin, meaning the 'ninth child'.

Nora: A variant of 'Eleanora', 'Honora' and 'Leonora'.

Noreen: Irish for 'Nora'.

Norma: From the Latin, meaning 'to rule'.

Octavia: From the Latin, meaning the 'eighth child'. The feminine form of 'Octavius'.

Octavie: French for 'Octavia'.

Odelia: From the old Norman French, meaning 'wealthy'.

Odell: From the Teutonic, meaning 'of the home'.

Odette: From the Teutonic, meaning 'of the home'.

Odille: From the Germanic, meaning 'of the fatherland'.

Olga: From the Russian, meaning 'holy'.

Olimpia: Italian for 'Olympia'.

Olive: From the Latin, meaning 'like the olive tree'.

Olivia: From the Latin, meaning 'like the olive tree'.

Olympe: French for 'Olympia'.

Olympie: German for 'Olympia'.

Ona: From the Latin, meaning 'as one'.

Oona: Irish for 'Ona'.

Oonagh: Irish for 'Ona'.

Ophelia: From the Greek, meaning 'help'. Example: *Ophelia* in 'Hamlet'.

Ophélie: French for 'Ophelia'.

Oriana: From the Latin, meaning 'golden'.

Orlanda: Italian for 'Rolanda'.

Orsola: Italian for 'Ursula'.

Ortensia: Italian for 'Hortense'.

Ottavia: Italian for 'Octavia'.

Ottilie: A variant of 'Odelia'.

Pamela: From the Greek, meaning 'honey'. A variant is *Pam*.

Pandora: From the Greek, meaning 'gifted'. Pandora's box is mentioned in Greek mythology, and was said to have contained all the troubles in the world, which escaped when the box was opened, except one - HOPE!

Pansy: From the French 'pensée', meaning a 'thought'.

Paola: Italian for 'Paula'.

Pat and **Pattie:** Variants of 'Patricia'.

Patience: Meaning 'one who endures'.

Patrice: French for 'Patricia'.

Patricia: From the Latin, meaning 'noble'. Variants are *Pat*, *Pansy* and *Pattie*.

Patrizia: Italian for 'Patricia'.

Patsy: An Irish variant of 'Patricia'.

Paula: The feminine form of 'Paul', meaning 'small'.

Paulette: French for 'Paula'.

Paulina: Spanish for 'Paula'.

Pauline: From the Latin, meaning 'small'.

Pearl: From the Latin, meaning a 'pearl'.

Peg and **Peggy:** Variants of 'Margaret'.

Penelope: From the Greek, meaning 'one who waves'. A variant is *Penny*.

Penny: A variant of 'Penelope'.

Peony: From the Latin, meaning the 'healer'.

Persephone: Meaning 'named after the goddess Persephone'.

Petra: From the Latin, meaning a 'rock'.

Petrina: A feminine form of 'Peter'.

Petronella: From the Latin, meaning a 'rock'.

Petronille: German for 'Petra'.

Petunia: Meaning 'like the petunia flower'.

Phil: A diminutive of 'Philippa'.

Philipine: German for 'Philippa'.

Philippa: The feminine form of 'Philip', meaning a 'horse lover'.

Philomena: From the Greek, meaning 'moon lover'.

Phoebe: From the Greek, meaning 'bright'.

Phyllis: From the Greek, meaning 'greenery'. A variant is *Phyll*.

Pierette: French for 'Petra'.

Polly: A variant of 'Mary', meaning 'bitter'.

Pollyanna: A combination of 'Polly' and 'Anna'.

Poppy: Meaning 'like the flower of this name'.

Portia: From the Latin, meaning a 'gift'. Portia was a leading character in Shakespeare's 'Merchant of Venice'.

Primrose: Meaning 'one who is like this flower'.

Priscilla: From the Latin, meaning 'ancient' (Acts 18.2). Variants are *Pris* and *Prissie*.

Prissie: A variant of 'Priscilla'.

Prudence: From the Latin, meaning 'foresighted'.

Prue: A diminutive of 'Prudence'.

Prunella: From the French 'Prunella', meaning 'prune coloured'.

Psyche: From the Greek, meaning 'of the soul'.

Queenie: From the Anglo Saxon, meaning 'like a queen'.

Querida: From the Spanish, meaning 'beloved'.

Quintina: A feminine form of 'Quintin', meaning the 'fifth child'.

Rachel: From the Hebrew, meaning a 'ewe'. Example: *Rachel the wife of Jacob.*

Rachele: Italian for 'Rachel'.

Rachelle: French for 'Rachel'.

Rahel: German for 'Rachel'.

Ramona: From the Spanish, meaning the 'wise one'.

Rani and **Ranee:** From the Hindi, meaning a 'queen'.

Raquel: Spanish for 'Rachel'.

Ray: A variant of 'Rachel'.

Rea: From the Greek, meaning 'in a stream'. This name is mentioned in the records of Somerset House (1905).

Rebeca: Spanish for 'Rebecca'.

Rébecca: French for 'Rebecca'.

Rebecca: From the Hebrew, meaning 'one who is bound'. A variant is *Becky*. Examples: *Rebecca, the wife of Isaac, Becky Sharp.*

Rebekka: Swedish and German for 'Rebecca'.

Regan: A variant of 'Regina', meaning 'queen'.

Regina: From the Latin, meaning 'like a queen'. Example: *Victoria Regina.*

Reina: Spanish for 'queen'.

Reine: French for 'queen'.

Rena: A variant of 'Renata'. From the Latin, meaning 'reborn'. This name is mentioned in the records in Somerset House, London (1903).

Renata: From the Latin, meaning 'reborn'.

Renate: German for 'Renata'.

Rene: A diminutive of 'Irene'. From the Greek, meaning 'peace'.

Renée: French for 'Renata'.

Rhoda: From the Greek, meaning a 'rose'.

Rhodia: From the Greek, meaning a 'rose'.

Rita: From 'Margarita', meaning a 'pearl'.

Roberta: The feminine form of 'Robert', from the Anglo Saxon, meaning 'famous and brilliant'.

Robina: The feminine form of 'Robin', i.e. a variant of 'Robert', from the Anglo Saxon, meaning 'famous and brilliant'.

Robine: French for 'Roberta'.

Roderica: From the Teutonic, meaning 'mighty ruler'. The feminine form of 'Roderick'.

Rolanda: From the Teutonic, meaning 'from a famous land'. The feminine form of 'Roland'.

Rolande: French for 'Rolanda'.

Roma: Meaning 'one who comes from Rome'.

Rosa: From the Latin, meaning 'like a rose'. Spanish, Italian, Danish, Swedish and Dutch for 'Rose'. Example: *Rosa Bonheur*.

Rosabel: Meaning a 'beautiful rose'. A combination of 'Rose' and 'Belle'.

Rosalie: From the Latin, meaning 'like a rose'. A variant is *Rosa*. Rosalie is the Patron Saint of Sicily.

Rosalind: From the Spanish, meaning 'like a beautiful rose'. A variant is *Rosa*. Rosalind was a character in 'As You like It' by Shakespeare.

Rosalinda: From the Spanish, meaning 'like a beautiful rose'.

Rosaline: A variant of 'Rosalind'.

Rosamond: Means 'protector of the rose'.

Rosamund: A variant of 'Rosamond'.

Rosamunda: Spanish for 'Rosamond'.

Rosanna: A combination of 'Rose' and 'Anna'.

Rose: Meaning 'like a rose'.

Rosemary: Meaning 'as sweet as the rosemary'. A variant is Rose Marie.

Rosemonde: French for 'Rosamond'.

Rosetta: A variant of 'Rose'.

Rosette: French for 'Rose'.

Rosie: A variant of 'Rose'.

Rosina: A variant of 'Rose'.

Rosita: Spanish for 'Rose'.

Rosmunda: Italian for 'Rosamond'.

Rowena: From the Anglo Saxon, meaning 'delightful and famous'.

Roxanne: From the Persian, meaning 'brilliant'.

Roxie: A variant of 'Roxanne'.

Rozamond: Dutch for 'Rosamond'.

Ruby: From the French, meaning 'like a ruby'.

Ruperta: German for 'Roberta'.

Ruth: From the Hebrew, meaning a 'friend' (Ruth 3.4).

Sabina: From the Latin, meaning a 'Sabine woman'.

Sabine: German, Dutch and French for 'Sabina'.

Sabrina: Meaning a 'seventh nymph'. Example: *'Sabrina Fair'* by Samuel Taylor.

Sadie: A variant of 'Sarah'. From the Hebrew, meaning a 'princess'.

Sal and **Sally:** Variants of 'Sarah'. Example: *'Sally Lunn'*.

Salome: From the Hebrew, meaning 'peace'. A variant is *Sal*. In the Bible Salome was the daughter of Herodias.

Samantha: Means 'one who listens'.

Sandie: A variant of 'Alexandra'.

Sandra: A variant of 'Alexandra'. From the Greek, meaning a 'helper'.

Sapphira: From the Hebrew, meaning 'beautiful' (Acts 5.1). Also meaning 'one who is like a sapphire'.

Sapphire: A variant of 'Sapphira'.

Sara: German, French, Italian and Spanish for 'Sarah'.

Sarah: From the Hebrew, meaning a 'princess'. Variants are *Sal*, *Sally* and *Sadie*. Sarah was the wife of Abraham. Examples: *Sarah Siddons*, *Sarah Bernhardt*.

Sari: A variant of 'Sarah', meaning a 'princess'.

Sarra: Probably a variant of 'Sarah'. A name mentioned in the Patent Rolls.

Scarlett: From the Anglo Saxon, meaning a 'scarlet woman'.

Selena: From the Latin, meaning 'heavenly'.

Selene: A variant of 'Selena'.

Selina: From the Latin, meaning 'heavenly'. This name is mentioned in the records at Somerset House, London (1901).

Selinda: A variant of 'Selena'.

Selma: A feminine form of 'Anslem'.

Seraphina: From the Hebrew, meaning 'ardent'.

Seraphine: A variant of 'Seraphina'.

Serena: From the Latin, meaning 'calm'.

Shari: A variant of 'Sharon', meaning a 'princess'.

Sharon: From the Hebrew, meaning a 'princess'. Example: The Rose of Sharon.

Sheelah: From the Hebrew, meaning 'petition'.

Sheena: From the Irish Gaelic, meaning 'God is good'.

Sheila: From the Irish for 'Cecilia'.

Sheilah: Gaelic for 'Sheila'.

Shelagh: From the Irish form of 'Celia'.

Sheree: A variant of 'Charlotte'.

Sheryl: A variant of 'Shirley'.

Shirl: A variant of 'Shirley'.

Shirley: From this surname, and meaning 'one who lives by the shire meadow'. A variant is Shirl.

Sibeal: Irish for 'Sybil'.

Sibyl: From the Greek, meaning 'able to prophesy'. A variant is Sibby.

Sibylla: Dutch for 'Sybil'.

Sibylle: German and French for 'Sybil'.

Sidney: From the old English 'Sidony', and from this surname, meaning 'one who lives on a great island'.

Sidonia: From the Latin, meaning a 'girl from Sidon'.

Silvana: A variant of 'Sylvia' and 'Silvia'.

Silvia: From the Latin, meaning 'of the forest'.

Silvie: French for 'Sylvia'.

Simona: From the Hebrew, meaning 'hearer'. The feminine form of 'Simon'.

Simone: French for 'Simona'.

Siobhan: Irish for 'Judith'.

Sis: A variant of 'Cecilia'.

Sofie: French, Dutch and Danish for 'Sophie'.

Sonia: Russian for 'Sophia', meaning 'wise'.

Sonja: Russian and Scandinavian for 'Sophie'.

Sophia: From the Greek, meaning 'wise'.

Sophie: From the Greek, meaning 'wise'.

Stacey: A variant of 'Eustacia' and 'Anastasia'. From the Greek, meaning 'at the resurrection'.

Stasia: A variant of 'Anastasia'.

Steffi and Steffie: Variants of 'Stephanie'.

Stella: From the Latin, meaning a 'star'.

Stellina: A variant of 'Stella', meaning a 'star'. This name is mentioned in the records of Somerset House, London (1905).

Stephanie: From the French, and the feminine of 'Stephen'. From the Greek, meaning 'crowned with a garland'.

Sukey: An old name for 'Susan'. From the Hebrew, meaning 'lily'.

Susan: From the Hebrew, meaning a 'lily'. Variants are *Sue* and *Susie*.

Susanna: Spanish for 'Susan'.

Susanne: German and French for 'Susan'.

Sussanna: Italian for 'Susan', and a name mentioned in the records of Somerset House, London (1904).

Sybil: From the Greek, meaning 'able to prophesy'. A variant is *Sibby.*

Sylvia: From the Latin, meaning 'of the forest'. A variant is *Sylvie.*

Syvilla: A variant of 'Sylvia', meaning 'of the forest'.

Tabitha: From the Hebrew, meaning a 'gazelle'.

Tallulah: From the Indian, meaning 'water leap'.

Tamara: From the Hebrew, meaning 'like a palm tree'.

Tammie: A variant of 'Tamara'.

Tammy: A feminine form of 'Thomas'.

Tara: From the Irish, meaning 'rocky'.

Teodora: Spanish and Italian for 'Theodora'.

Teodosia: Italian for 'Theodosia'.

Teresa: From the Greek, meaning 'one who reaps'. Spanish and Italian for 'Theresa'.

Terese: A variant of 'Teresa'.

Terri: A variant of 'Theresa'.

Terry: A variant of 'Theresa', meaning 'one who reaps.'

Tess: A variant of 'Tessa'. Example: *'Tess Of The D'Urbervilles'*.

Tessa: A variant of 'Teresa', meaning 'one who reaps'.

Tessie: A variant of 'Tessa'.

Thea: A variant of 'Althea'.

Theda: A variant of 'Theodora'.

Thelma: From the Greek, meaning a 'small child'.

Theodora: From the Greek, meaning 'God's gift'.

Theodosia: From the Greek, meaning 'God's gift'.

Theresa: From the Greek, meaning 'one who reaps'. Variants are *Terry, Tessa, Tracey*. Example: *St. Theresa*.

Thérèse: French for 'Theresa'.

Therese: German for 'Theresa'.

Thirza: From the Hebrew, meaning 'pleasant'. This name is mentioned in the records in Somerset House, London (1906).

Thomasina: A feminine form of 'Thomas' (usually found in Scotland).

Thora: From the Norse god 'Thor' (the god of thunder).

Tilda: A variant of 'Mathilda'.

Tilly: A variant of 'Mathilda'.

Tina: A diminutive of 'Christina'.

Titania: From the Greek, meaning a 'giant'. Titania was the queen of the fairies in Shakespeare's 'Midsummer Night's Dream'.

Toni: A variant of 'Antonia'.

Tonia: A variant of 'Antonia', meaning 'without price'.

Tracey: A variant of 'Theresa'.

Tracy: From the Irish, meaning a 'fighter'.

Trixie: A variant of 'Beatrice', meaning 'joy bringer'.

Trudie: A variant of 'Gertrude'.

Trudy: From the Teutonic, meaning 'one who is loved'.

Ulrica: A feminine form of 'Ulric', meaning 'wolf's ruler'. This name is mentioned in the records of Somerset House, London (1901).

Una: From the Latin, meaning 'together'.

Ursola: Spanish for 'Ursula'.

Ursula: From the Latin, meaning a 'she bear'.

Ursule: French for 'Ursula'.

Val: A diminutive of 'Valerie', meaning 'strong one'. From the old French.

Valda: From the Scandinavian, meaning a 'ruler'.

Valentia: A variant of 'Valentina', meaning 'strong'.

Valentina: From the Latin, meaning 'strong'.

Valeria: Italian for 'Valerie'.

Valerie: From the old French, meaning 'strong one'. A variant is *Val*.

Vallie: A variant of 'Valerie'.

Vanessa: Means 'handsome'.

Vangie: A variant of 'Evangeline'.

Vania: A variant of 'Vanessa'.

Vashti: From the Persian, meaning 'beautiful'. In the Bible Queen Vashti was the wife of King Asaheurus (Esther 1.9).

Velda: From the Scandinavian, meaning a 'ruler'.

Venetia: Meaning 'one who comes from Venice'.

Vera: From the Russian, meaning 'faithful'.

Veronica: From the Greek, meaning 'victorious'.

Veronike: German for 'Bernice'.

Veronique: French for 'Bernice'.

Vesta: From 'Vesta', the Roman goddess of fire.

Vicki and **Vicky:** A variant of 'Victoria'. From the Latin, meaning 'victory'.

Victoire: French for 'Victoria'

Victoria: From the Latin, meaning 'victory'.

Vida: From the Spanish, meaning 'life'.

Vilhelmina: Swedish for 'Wilhelmina'.

Vilma: A variant of 'Wilhelmina'.

Viola: From the Latin, meaning 'violet'. A variant is Vi.

Violante: Spanish for 'Violet'.

Viole: French for 'Violet'.

Violet: From the Latin, meaning 'violet'. A variant is Vi.

Violetta: Italian for 'Violet'.

Violette: A variant of 'Violet'.

Virginia: From the Latin, meaning a 'virgin'. Variants are Ginny and Ginger.

Virginie: Dutch and French for 'Virginia'.

Vitoria: Spanish for 'Victoria'.

Vittoria: Italian for 'Victoria'.

Viv: A variant of 'Vivien'.

Viviana: A variant of 'Vivien'.

Vivien: From the Latin, meaning 'lively'. A variant is Viv.

Wanda: From the Teutonic, meaning a 'wanderer'.

Wenda: From the Teutonic, meaning a 'wanderer'.

Wendy: From the Teutonic, meaning a 'wanderer'. Example: *Wendy is the heroine in 'Peter Pan' by J.M. Barrie.*

Wendyl: A variant of 'Wendy'.

Wilhelmina: From the Teutonic, meaning 'bold protector'. Variants are *Ina* and *Willa*.

Wilhelmine: Danish for 'Wilhelmina'.

Willa: A variant of 'Wilhelmina'.

Williamina: A variant of 'Wilhelmina' (often used in Scotland). Variants are *Willa* and *Ina*.

Wilma: A variant of 'Wilhelmina'.

Winifred: From the Teutonic, meaning 'friend of peace'. Variants are *Win* and *Winnie*.

Winnie: A variant of 'Winifred', meaning 'friend of peace'.

Xanthe: From the Greek, meaning 'golden or yellow haired'.

Xanthippe: The wife of Socrates, who is said to have been of a quarrelsome disposition.

Xaviera: From the Spanish, meaning 'new house owner'. The feminine form of 'Xavier'.

Xenia: From the Greek, meaning 'hospitable'.

Yetta: A variant of 'Henrietta', meaning 'ruler of the home'.

Yolande: From the Greek, meaning a 'violet'. French for 'Violet'.

Yolanthe: A variant of 'Yolande'.

Ysabel: Spanish for 'Elizabeth'.

Yseult: From the Welsh, meaning 'one who is fair'.

Ysobel: A variant of 'Isobel'.

Yvette: From the Norman French, meaning 'like a yew bow'.

Yvonne: From the Norman French, meaning 'like a yew bow'.

Zara: From the Hebrew, meaning 'bright as the dawn'.

Zelda: A variant of 'Griselda'.

Zelia: From the Greek, meaning 'zealous'.

Zelma: From the old Norse 'Anselm'.

Zena: A variant of 'Zenobia'. From the Greek, meaning 'given life by the god Zeus'.

Zenia: A variant of 'Zenobia'.

Zenobia: From the Greek, meaning 'given life by the god Zeus'.

Zénobie: French for 'Zenobia'.

Zeta: From the sixth letter of the Greek alphabet, and the name given to a sixth born child.

Zilla: From the Hebrew, meaning a 'shadow'.

Zita: A variant of 'Theresa'.

Zöe: From the Greek, meaning 'life'.

Zona: From the Latin, meaning a 'girdle'.

Zora: From the Arabic, meaning 'dawn'.

Zsa-Zsa: The Hungarian form of 'Susan'.

In the same series...

THE EXPECTANT FATHER

Betty Parsons is a legend. Her outstanding authority stems from her professional training as a nurse and over 30 years of ante-natal classes showing mothers-to-be and their husbands how to share the magic of childbirth through *understanding*.

This deliberately dad-centred book prepares dad to maximise his support from the beginning.

As Betty masterminds your joint progress, any private worries you may have will be assuaged and the daily crop of questions about the mechanics of labour which besieges every couple will be resolved. Above all, Betty instills the conviction - so precious when the birth day arrives - that you will both ride safely above the natural fears with which every mother must cope when facing such a new and challenging experience.

Uniform with this book.

ELLIOT RIGHT WAY BOOKS KINGSWOOD, SURREY, U.K.

In the same series . . .

GOING ON TO SOLIDS

(Feeding baby: from four months)

- ★ When should I start offering solids?
- ★ What type of food should I offer?
- ★ How much should I give and how often?
- ★ What is the best time to give solids?
- ★ What should I do when baby rejects the food?
- ★ When should baby begin feeding himself?

This book is the answer to these and many other questions. It gives the technique of tempting baby on to solid foods. But that is just the start . . .

The main part of the book consists of more than 180 appetising recipes which are simple to make and inexpensive, and can be freshly prepared whenever required. The comprehensive range includes purées, soups, fish and meat dishes, desserts and beverages so that you can nurture your baby through weaning and on to a well-balanced, additive-free diet.

ELLIOT RIGHT WAY BOOKS KINGSWOOD, SURREY, U.K.

Uniform with this book

SOLD - WITH OR WITHOUT AN ESTATE AGENT

Nicolas Savage writes with the experience of his successful years in an estate agency partnership. He details the widespread inefficiencies, alerts you to the temptations that confront every agent, and reveals the right way to handle delicate 'chains'. Read how to select the best agent and work constructively together. Or, if you want to sell privately, discover the exact procedures to follow. Learn to *buy* as well.

This lively and controversial book sets out all the secrets known to the Professionals in terms that everybody can understand.

What to Watch out for When
BUYING OR SELLING A HOUSE

Michael Llewelyn has spent many years in estate agency, and is a Fellow of the Royal Institution of Chartered Surveyors. He gives comprehensive coverage of the legal and financial pitfalls which beset the home buyer and seller. Learn where to go, and when, whom to see, how much to offer or ask, and how much to spend.

ELLIOT RIGHT WAY BOOKS
KINGSWOOD, SURREY, U.K.

OTHER GREAT PAPERFRONT BOOKS

Each uniform with this book

FOOD PROCESSORS PROPERLY EXPLAINED

Dianne Page shows how to make the most of your food processor. As well as giving full details of how to look after and use this kitchen wizard, the author gives standard procedures for processing vegetables, meat, purées, ice-cream, pastries, bread, cakes (and icing), plus ten wonderful chapters of delicious recipes.

SLOW COOKING PROPERLY EXPLAINED

Slow cookers develop the rich flavours that make tender roasts, tasty soups, stews and casseroles. Pâtés, sponges and mulled wine can also be prepared in them. Even fish and delicate fruits and vegetables can be gently cooked and remain whole after long cooking. Dianne Page explains this economical and flexible method of cooking and provides an assortment of over 100 recipes.

PRESSURE COOKING PROPERLY EXPLAINED

Pressure cookers are straightforward, giving excellent results - useful for preserves, everyday meals and dinner parties. Dianne Page explains how to use them to their best advantage. Time-consuming recipes can be prepared cheaply and conveniently. Cheaper cuts of meat can be tenderised quickly and the flavours and nutritional value of foods are retained. Includes a wide variety of recipes.

ELLIOT RIGHT WAY BOOKS
KINGSWOOD, SURREY, U.K.

Joke books in the same series:

JOKES FOR TELLING

Here are over 600 jokes in A to Z subject order, compiled by Kevin Goldstein-Jackson who has written for a number of top TV comedians. An added feature is the special Joke Directory, enabling you to call up *all* the jokes on the subject you want fast. You can thus guarantee yourself an audience rolling about during after-dinner speeches or wedding receptions. See how quicky you can find the required dose of laughter!

THE RIGHT JOKE FOR THE RIGHT OCCASION
also by Kevin Goldstein-Jackson

There's no need to be left out or tongue-tied if you dig into this mine of humour. Here is the recipe for laughter (and the cure for groans). Over 600 jokes. Whether you are searching for a joke about the birds and the bees, or about camels, cars or cats, you should find it here.

JOKE . . . AFTER JOKE . . . AFTER JOKE
also by Kevin Goldstein-Jackson

Has over 600 jokes in a handy ABC order, *plus* a brilliant subject suitability directory − here is laughter on tap. Quick quips and side splitters will have your friends bent double, helplessly beseeching you to stop unleashing joke . . . after joke . . . after joke.

ELLIOT RIGHT WAY BOOKS
KINGSWOOD, SURREY, U.K.

OUR PUBLISHING POLICY

HOW WE CHOOSE

Our policy is to consider every deserving manuscript and we can give special editorial help where an author is an authority on his subject but an inexperienced writer. We are rigorously selective in the choice of books we publish. We set the highest standards of editorial quality and accuracy. This means that a *Paperfront* is easy to understand and delightful to read. Where illustrations are necessary to convey points of detail, these are drawn up by a subject specialist artist from our own panel.

HOW WE KEEP PRICES LOW

We aim for the big seller. This enables us to order enormous print runs and achieve the lowest price for you. Unfortunately, this means that you will not find in the *Paperfront* list any titles on obscure subjects of minority interest only. These could not be printed in large enough quantities to be sold for the low price at which we offer this series. We sell almost all our *Paperfronts* at the same unit price. This saves a lot of fiddling about in our clerical departments and helps us to give you world-beating value. Under this system, the longer titles are offered at a price which we believe to be unmatched by any publisher in the world.

OUR DISTRIBUTION SYSTEM

Because of the competitive price, and the rapid turnover, *Paperfronts* are possibly the most profitable line a bookseller can handle. They are stocked by the best bookshops all over the world. It may be that your bookseller has run out of stock of a particular title. If so, he can order more from us at any time - we have a fine reputation for 'same day' despatch, and we supply any order, however small (even a single copy), to any bookseller who has an account with us. We prefer you to buy from your bookseller, as this reminds him of the strong underlying public demand for *Paperfronts*. Members of the public who live in remote places, or who are housebound, or whose local bookseller is unco-operative, can order direct from us by post.

FREE

If you would like an up-to-date list of all *Paperfront* titles currently available, send a stamped self-addressed envelope to:
ELLIOT RIGHT WAY BOOKS, BRIGHTON ROAD, LOWER KINGSWOOD, SURREY, U.K.